COME
REMINISCE WITH ME

Stories of Growing Up in the 1930's
in the Midwest

By Dr. Emmett Murray
("Duke" Murray)

Ft. Myers, Florida

Printed in Victoria, Canada

National Library of Canada Cataloguing in Publication Data

Murray, Emmett, 1925-
        Come reminisce with me / Emmett Murray.
ISBN 1-4120-0981-2
        I. Title.
F499.L73M87 2004   977.1'42'092   C2003-904300-2

TRAFFORD

This book was published *on-demand* in cooperation with Trafford Publishing. On-demand publishing is a unique process and service of making a book available for retail sale to the public taking advantage of on-demand manufacturing and Internet marketing. **On-demand publishing** includes promotions, retail sales, manufacturing, order fulfilment, accounting and collecting royalties on behalf of the author.

Suite 6E, 2333 Government St., Victoria, B.C. V8T 4P4, CANADA

Phone	250-383-6864	Toll-free	1-888-232-4444 (Canada & US)
Fax	250-383-6804	E-mail	sales@trafford.com
Web site	www.trafford.com	TRAFFORD PUBLISHING IS A DIVISION OF TRAFFORD HOLDINGS LTD.	
Trafford Catalogue #03-1350		www.trafford.com/robots/03-1350.html	

10   9   8   7   6   5   4   3   2   1

Our Old Neighborhood

in Lima, Ohio

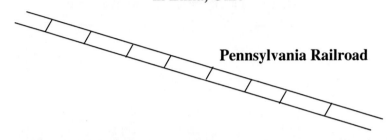

Pennsylvania Railroad

HUTCHINSONS	SPEIDEL, then WARNER Family	MURRAYS	ANDERSONS	CREVISTONS
1170	1164	1158	1152	1146

W   *HAZEL AVENUE*   **E**

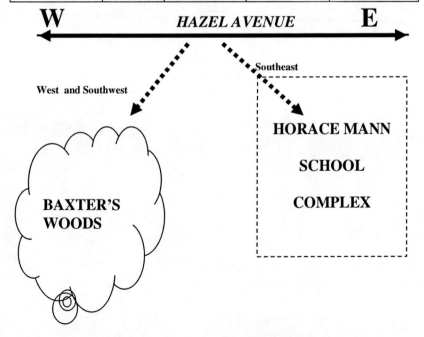

Southeast

West and Southwest

BAXTER'S
WOODS

HORACE MANN

SCHOOL

COMPLEX

i

The Hazel Avenue Murrays

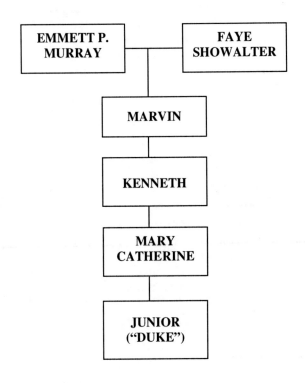

EMMETT P. MURRAY

FAYE SHOWALTER

MARVIN

KENNETH

MARY CATHERINE

JUNIOR ("DUKE")

Acknowledgements

The task of assembling all of my manuscripts into an orderly form has seemed mountainous to me. I have so many family members and friends, old and new, to thank, I scarcely know where to start.

Thanks to my dear wife and best friend, Polly, who read my handwritten stories to me as I typed them, and corrected my spelling and punctuation as we went along. Not only that, but she read most of my stories aloud to the memoirs group.

Thanks to son, Robb, who has kept my eye on the ball to complete this project, put me on the internet, and helped me in so many ways.

Thanks to Scott Murray and Nancy Winters, Betsy and Steve Fowler, and Cindy and Steve Hamblen for their encouragement and help. Nancy Winters encouraged my efforts from their earliest days, Steve Fowler proofread with his printer's eye and Steve Hamblen led by example in writing an autobiography several years ago.

Most hearty thanks as well to Alene Grothouse, Esther Stover Gorman, Peg Wise, Dr. Dixie Davis, Dr. William F. Foxx, Betty Negelspach, Dr. and Mrs. Earl McGovern, Jack and Glenna McCullough and family, Dr. Dennis K. Burns, and Dr. and Mrs. A.C. Reed for their encouragement.

Special thanks to Jean Engstrom for her appreciation and encouragement, and for help in researching details. For additional details and

Acknowledgements

informa-tion I would also like to thank my cousin Dorothy Neu, sister-in-law Sudie Loman Murray, and my beloved sister, Mary Kuskowski.

I would like to express particular gratitude to my cousin, Roberta Rodabaugh, for help with facts and specifics, and especially for her kind permission to use several of her family photos in this book.

Thank you also to Deborah Hawkins, Alison Walsh and Amy Lund, all fine editors, who helped as test readers to put many finishing touches on the book prior to publication. I am grateful as well for the supportive and helpful comments of Terrence Gargiulo (author of *Making Stories*) and for the example of Denise Garon Miller in publishing her marvelous autobiography (*Swing Girl*, Mama Shoe Press, 2002).

Thanks to Noel and Bert MacCarry for their instructions in storytelling.

Thanks to Phyllis G. Bailey-Stormer who encouraged me and instructed me in our Memoirs Class.

And lastly, thanks to all the members of our Memoirs course who put up with my trying out my stories on them.

--Dr. Emmett Murray, Jr., M.D.

MY STORIES:

vi

Dedication

This book is for all the people -- family members, relatives, neighbors, school teachers and Sunday school teachers -- who made up the milieu in which I grew up in Lima.

This book is for my wife, Pauline (Polly) Murray, who played such a vital role in its production, as did our son, Robb Murray. It is for our children, Scott, Robb, Cindy, and Betsy, and for their mates, Nancy Winters, Steve Hamblen, and Steve Fowler, and for our grandchildren, Drew, Chris, Kim and Jeff.

It is also for my sister, Mary, and her husband Val Kuskowski. It is for my cousins, Roberta Rodabaugh, Dorothy Neu, Betty Negelspach, Martha Sloan, Jim and Jack Morrison, and Ellen Jenkins.

This book is in memory of my parents, Emmett P. and Mary F. (Showalter) Murray, Uncle Charles and Aunt Lu (Showalter) Shilling, Uncle Ray and Aunt Lydia Murray. It is also in honor of my two brothers: Marvin who guided me through high school and into college, and Kenneth, who got his Purple Heart the hard way and missed connecting with me in England.

It is also in memory of the wonderful teachers I had at Horace Mann School and, throughout the years, those I also had at Lima Central.

This book is for my classmates still living, and for those who have passed on.

This book is also for the Allen County Historical Museum, and the curator, Pat Smith, staff

1

and docents, and for Jean Engstrom, whose enthusiastic columns about the book in the *Lima News* really helped to get the word out. Jean is a very special and most valued friend. This book is also for the Lima City School System which gave us all an excellent education. Many of us didn't realize what a great education we had received until some time after graduation.

If this book stirs your memories and brings forth a smile or two, then it has served its purpose.

--Dr. Emmett Murray, Jr., M.D.

Foreword:
Come Reminisce with Me

I was born on August 18, 1925, at my family's home at 1158 Hazel Avenue in Lima, Ohio. My father, a master carpenter, had built the house himself around 1914. I believe that all four of the kids in our family were born at home in that same house. I know that I was a breech delivery, attended by Dr. Stadler, and my Aunt Lydia Murray was in attendance for Mom.

My birth certificate read "Emmett Junior Murray", and throughout grade school I was known as Junior Murray. I had some teasing older cousins, such as Dorothy Neu, who used to call me Biddy (like a little "biddy hen". Biddies were chickens of small breed and some farmers kept them around more or less as pets and curiosities. Some people called them Banties – for example, Banty roosters and hens. I have to confess that sometimes my mom when in a jesting mood also called me Biddy.).

My oldest brother, Marvin, learned in a course of heraldry that the youngest son of a Baron was a Duke. Marvin was given to grand expressions and, since I was the youngest in our family, he started calling me Duke. And, by golly, it stuck.

I've had other names and titles, too, such as Private Emmett (nmi) Murray, Jr. The (nmi) stood for "no mid-dle initial." Later I moved up to Sgt. Murray. After the Army and my return to college, I eventually became known as Doctor Murray.

3

While being a doctor, I served at various times as Chief of Staff for two hospitals and, for a while, as President of the Lima City School Board.

Once I retired from practice, I took the training and became a docent at the Lima and Allen County Historical Museum. While a docent, I decided to try my hand at writing and, after doing some reading and re-search in Dr. Don English's book, *The Gauze Curtain*, I wrote a piece about the first doctor in Allen County to refer to when explaining our museum's Medical Display.

I liked it – writing, that is, so when Polly and I settled here at the Woodlands in Shell Point Village, I joined a class in memoir writing. I wanted to tell our children how things were when I was growing up -- and hopefully in a humorous manner because I feel that humor is essential to our well-being. Without humor, none of the poor souls who survived the Nazi concentration camps would have made it.

As I have read in other books about the period from 1925 to 1941 and the advent of WW II, which is the era I am writing about, America was in a severe depression. I know that times were tough, but I could never remember my father's being out of work. We were fortunate, but very scaled-back. I never went without warm clothes or shoes. But shoe repair shops were numerous, and when something wore out, we repaired it, and made do.

As kids back then, we didn't have too much trouble finding jobs for making our spending money, and we were careful how we spent that money. I don't ever recall getting an allowance, but still never felt deprived.

Since I began these memoirs, they have not only been well-received by our kids, but also by friends and acquaintances we have made. At the end of the memoirs, I have included the original story about "The First Doctor in Allen County" that got me started on this project.

I hope that you will enjoy these memories as much as I have, recalling the trials, tribulations and joys of growing up in the small Midwestern town of Lima, Ohio in the 1930's.

--Dr. Emmett "Duke" Murray, Jr., M.D.

DISCLAIMER: All facts mentioned in these stories are simply presented as the best of my recollection. Any mistakes, omissions or misstatements are completely unintentional. If you will bring any errors noted to my attention, I will make an immediate correction for the next edition. We are planning small press runs only, so this will be no problem. Please contact me at
           dukepollyfm@webtv.net

Days of Innocence

Age 3

7

1. Two Young Boys Discover Fire

(or, *How Not to Boil Eggs*)

Back in 1931 or thereabouts, my closest friend was Bobby Creviston. I lived at 1158 Hazel Avenue in Lima, Ohio, and the Crevistons lived at 1146. (A lawyer named Perry Anderson lived between Bob's house and mine – please see the map on page i at the front of the book.)

Bob's dad was a heavy smoker (Lucky Strike Green) and there was always a liberal supply of matches and a newfangled cigarette lighter on the smoking stand beside his easy chair. In the summer, when things were slow at the lumberyard Mr. Creviston ran (just two blocks away from his home), he would come home in the afternoon and sit down in his chair. There, he would smoke and listen to the play-by-play broadcast of Detroit Tigers baseball, or any game he could bring in on his Stewart-Warner radio. (These would be afternoon games as there were no night games back then.)

One morning when I was about five years old, I was over at the Crevistons and up in Bob's room with him. He wanted to show me a new cigarette lighter that his dad had acquired. To demonstrate how to use it, he pressed down on a lever to strike a light. But a stream of flame shot out, hit his curtains and caught them on fire!

As soon as I saw the flames start, I flew downstairs and found Mrs. Creviston, and told her

9

about the fire, and she bolted upstairs -- at least, as fast as her polio-impaired legs could take her. She pulled down the curtains, rolled them up and extinguished the flames.

I realized that the situation was under control, but also that the Creviston household was no place for me to be at that moment. Mr. Creviston was a stern-looking man and I knew that Bob was in for it. So I beat a hasty retreat out the front door, leaped off the porch, and headed home. Naturally, my mom found out what had happened, and Bob's house was off-limits for me until further notice. Also, my playing with Bob at all was on probation for quite a while.

Several months later, in mid-October, Bob and I were off probation and allowed to play together again. We were in his back yard and we wandered over into the back yard of his neighbors to the east. Back then, many people had chicken coops in their back yards, to raise a few hens for eggs and an occasional fryer. But all the chicken coops in our block, including the Murrays', were defunct. We used ours for a dog kennel, and the Crevistons and the Andersons had torn theirs down.

Bob and I wandered into the neighbor's chicken coop and found several nests with old, dry straw in them. Bob remarked, "If we had the ingredients, we could make some hard-boiled eggs!" That adventure sounded good to two boys six year olds, so Bob slipped into his kitchen and got a pan full of water, several eggs and some matches.

According to him, we could just set the pan containing the water and eggs into the nest, light the straw with a match and, *"Presto!"*, we would have hard-boiled eggs. It sounded okay to me and, after all, Bob was older (by six months) and already in the second grade (thanks to his teacher mother's accelerated plans for him). So, we proceeded.

Well, Mrs. Creviston looked out of her upstairs bedroom window towards the glassless window of her neighbor's chicken coop just as the first billows of smoke started to roll out. It didn't take her long to realize that there was trouble afoot, and that Bob and that Murray kid must be in back of it. She rang up the fire department and it was but a short time before we heard sirens and bells coming.

Bob and I scooted back over into his back yard and tried to become invisible against the foundation of his house. The fire crew soon dispatched the fire, but the chicken coop had seen its last days and was totally destroyed.

Fire Chief John Mack was a large, tall man with steel gray hair and a full mustache to match. He had icy blue eyes that really set off his white Fire Chief's cap. Someone directed him over to where Bob and I were cowering.

Bob must have cowered better than I because the one Chief Mack looked down at most sternly was me. He reached out, gently grasped my chin, and opened my mouth. He peered inside, closed it up again, and said, "I thought I might see a burned match in there, but I didn't. Did you swallow it?" I shook my head vigorously in the negative.

He then moved over to Bob for the same examination. Then he said that he thought that our mothers could continue the rest of this investigation to a satisfactory conclusion. As he walked back to the fire truck, I was very much relieved because I fully expected him to scoop me up and take me downtown to the police station, which happened to be right next to the fire station.

Well, Bob and I were back on probation again. And I don't know *when* we ended up getting back together *that* time. . .

Several years later, Fire Chief John Mack died and was interred in a mausoleum in the Woodlawn Cemetery. Every summer, Bob and I would ride our bikes out there and go into the mausoleum and stare with awe at the marble tablet that had the inscription, "Captain John Mack, Chief, Lima Fire Department."

And, of course, we always remembered how *not* to make hard-boiled eggs.

2. Lost in Buffalo

It was 1933. I was eight years old. The country was in a depression, although I did not realize it at the time. My father was a master carpenter and a construc-tion foreman. In my whole life, I cannot ever remember my father being out of work.

My mother was a financial genius, as she would stretch paychecks to the breaking point. As I remember, she bought insurance for ten cents a week and I can still remember Mr. Brown coming every Friday and collecting the dime and entering it in his debit book.

Mother didn't trust the banks then, and I remember her hiding a ten-dollar bill under the corner of the dining room carpet, or pulling down a window shade and rolling a 20-dollar bill up in it. She always said, "If there is a fire, grab the window shades and run outside."

At any rate, back in 1933, my dad's employer, The Green and Sawyer Company, took a subcontracting job on a big state hospital in the state of New York, just south of Buffalo, in a little town called Gowanda. Since it was so far from Lima, he rented a room there and would only come home once every six or eight weeks.

The second summer of the job, my folks were able to rent a furnished house there from a football coach who was going to be away taking college courses. So my mom loaded my two brothers, my sister and me into our 1928 Chrysler and we moved to Gowanda, New York for the summer.

13

My brothers were able to get local construction jobs for the summer, and so they were busy most of the time and had other interests.

One Saturday, my parents, sister and I, along with another couple from the construction team, the Agenbroads, took a trip to Buffalo, about 35 miles to the north. We parked the car a few blocks away from the main street and business district, and walked to busy downtown Buffalo.

We were walking by a big department store and my parents stopped to look at something in the window. I was investigating one of the sidewalk elevators that they used to take merchandise down from the curbside to the basement of the store.

Apparently, several people moved in behind my folks and, when I looked up, I couldn't see them. So off I took, looking for them, and the more I couldn't spot them, the faster I walked, and then I began to cry and call for my mom.

I was two or three blocks along when two Polish ladies, all dressed in black as if they had been to a funeral, grabbed hold of me, and I couldn't understand them and then I *did* start to bawl. They took me to a policeman on the corner and turned me over to him, and that *really* scared me!

The policeman blew his whistle, stopped the traffic, and walked me over to a patrol car parked across the street. He talked to the officer in the front seat, opened the back door, and put me inside. The officers calmed me down and said they would find my mom and dad.

Meanwhile, back at the department store, all hell broke loose when Mom turned around and I was gone. She was angry and frightened, and told the cop on the corner that she was going to "shake the socks off me when she got me back". But, just then, the patrol car, with me inside, pulled up to where she was standing. The officers got me out and she overflowed with tears and almost hugged me to pieces.

So she didn't shake my socks off -- but *I never went back to Buffalo again!*

3.   Foaming at the Mouth

As I previously explained, the summer of 1933 found the Murrays of Lima, Ohio living in a rented, furnished house in western New York State in the little town of Gowanda.

Living next door to us was an Italian family, the Gelias.   Rosa was the matriarch, or Momma, and Primo was an eight-year-old boy who became my inseparable friend.

We would play hard all day and, as evening approached, Rosa would come onto their front porch and shout "Primo, you come home now!" We would continue to play and I would say "Don't you have to go now?" and he would say "Not yet."

Then Rosa would come out and call out again, "Primo, come to supper!"   But Primo would say to me, "I don't have to go yet."   Then Rosa would come about five minutes later and shout *Primo, you come home right now or I give you the lick!*

"Now I gotta go!" he would say, and off he would run.

One Sunday, my folks were going to go to a nearby Indian Reservation and watch the Lacrosse games, and I got permission for Primo to go with us. People would park their cars at the side of the field and watch these rough games.   Primo and I would find other things to interest us and were left to our own pursuits.

16

There was a raspberry patch behind the cars, and so Primo and I became entrepreneurs. We would pull out the long stem of a timothy plant and carefully thread 15 or so raspberries onto the stem and when we had 15 or 20 stems ready, we would walk along the cars and sell our wares for a penny a stalk. We made enough penny-candy money to last us for several weeks.

One day, I was in the house, and Primo came by and asked my older brother, Ken, who was on the porch, if I was home. My brother called in to me and said that Primo was out front. Then he planted his foot down about a foot from the bottom of the screen door. I ran and pushed on the screen door and it flew back and hit me in the nose.

My brother laughed and I cut lose with some choice playground profanity.

I was suddenly jerked up by the collar of my shirt and marched to the kitchen sink. Mom told me to smile and show my teeth and then she took a soft bar of Fels naphtha soap and mashed it into my mouth and teeth. I was soon literally foaming at the mouth. Mom then took pity on me and took a toothbrush and helped get the soap out of the spaces between my teeth.

And as for Ken – well, he was six feet tall and weighed 225 pounds. So them was the breaks.

I never went out of that screen door again without thinking of my foaming at the mouth experience, and the horrible taste of Fels naphtha soap.

4.   Two Family Quests with My Sister, Mary

My two brothers, Marvin and Kenneth, were 10 and 8 years older than me, respectively. We were in semi-different generations and, sadly, both my brothers have now passed on.

My sister, Mary, still happily alive, is around 3 years older than me, and so we were closer to each other age-wise than our brothers. It was Mary's job to watch over me when I was a toddler playing in the front yard. She had to keep me from running out in the street and possibly getting hit by a car. It was also her job to bring me inside the house when Mom announced that supper was ready. I always resisted, but Mary always overcame my maneuvers and dragged me into the house.

According to my mom, Mary had chicken pox when she was six months old and it wasn't until a year or so later that they discovered it had affected her hearing. My parents took Mary to several doctors but there was no help to be had.

When I was about five, my parents heard of a world-renowned ear specialist in St. Louis and they made the necessary arrangements to go see him. We boarded the Nickel Plate passenger train headed for St. Louis, and off the four of us went: Mom, Dad, Mary -- and I, tagging along.

Again, there was no help for Mary's hearing in St. Louis, but while we were there, our folks took us to their famous zoo. The most memorable thing I saw there was a huge walrus or sea lion. When the trainer would walk up the walrus's back, it would tip its head back and the attendant would drop a whole fish into its open mouth. After four or five fish, the attendant would walk back down off its back and the walrus would bellow loudly. I asked Dad what the man had dropped into the sea lion's mouth and he said "some big sardines." That was the highlight of our trip to St. Louis, as far as I was concerned.

A couple of years later, my mom heard of an old lady who was a North American Indian Shaman or witch doctor. She was reported to have miraculous healing power. So off again the four of us went to a small rural town in southern Indiana.

We located the house where the lady lived and, after parking the car, we went up on the porch and knocked on the door. "Come in!" she said, and we entered into a darkened living room. My mom asked the shaman if she could do anything for Mary's hearing. She had Mary approach her and then she took a length of string from a typical cone of heavy grocery string. She would measure various diameters of Mary's head and tie a knot with each measurement.

She then threw the string into an old enameled pan and placed a flat rock on top of the pan. Next she took another length of string and made another set of measurements, and tied a knot at each mark, and then threw that string into the pan with the other strings.

19

This was done eight or nine times and suddenly Mary grabbed her ears and told Mom they hurt. Well, we thought we were going to witness a miracle, but it didn't happen. The Shaman said that it may take several weeks and not to give up hope.

Then the old lady looked at my Dad and said "Your feet hurt you, don't they?" Dad admitted that, several months before, he had fallen off a second floor scaffold and landed on his feet and they had bothered him ever since. She told him to get a certain kind of arch supports, which he later did when we got home, and he seemed to get some relief. As we were leaving, Mom put a "free will offering" into a bowl, which kept the old lady from practicing medicine without a license.

The Shaman murmured a word of thanks and then pointed at me and said, "He has pinworms. Get him some Dr. Jaynes Vermifuge: two doses a day for six months." Mom's mouth flew open and so did mine. I had just come along for the ride, but for the next six months I had to take that nasty-tasting medicine!

At that time, Mary was going to a class for the hearing-impaired at Faurot school. It was taught by a Mrs. Gratz, who lived in nearby Bluffton. After a year or so, the Superintendent of Schools closed the class because there were too few students.

Then Mrs. Gratz opened a private school in Findlay, about 35 miles from Lima. My folks made arrangements with a family there to give Mary board and room from Sunday night to Friday. We would pick Mary up each Friday afternoon for the weekend and then return her on Sunday evening.

This lasted about a year and, when this school closed, my parents were advised to enter Mary into the Ohio State School for the Deaf in Columbus. So, over the summer, arrangements were made for the next school year.

The next September, we took Mary down to the School on East Town Street in Columbus. There was a huge older building that held the dormitories, offices, kitchens and dining room. The school classrooms were in a separate building.

I remember the highly polished hardwood floors in the dormitories and the students happily pushing big dry dust mops around to polish the floors. There were no bunk beds, as I remember; each student had a little metal bed of his or her own.

Well, it came time for us to return home and Mary was to remain at the Deaf School. I remember Mom was crying, Mary was crying, I was crying, and Dad was blowing his nose. I cried all the way home, so Mom and Dad stopped in Marysville at an Isaly's store and got us each an ice cream cone. It helped for a while, but the ache of loneliness was still there.

As it turned out, it was the best thing for Mary, as she made many friends there. When she would come home in the summer, she would write letters to her friends and, as the summer ended, Mary was anxious to return to school and resume where things had ended in the spring. She not only met many girl friends there, but also met the man, Valerian Kuskowski, with whom she would live the rest of her life, and they have been married for 57 years, I believe.

And the profound things left on my young, impressionable mind from the trips of our Quests were two:

1) To this day, I cannot eat whole sardines and

2) I never prescribed Dr. Jayne's Vermifuge for any of my patients with pinworms -- or any *other* kind of worms!

5. Highway to Oklahoma

My last installment in my memoir collection was about "Tagging Along on Two Family Quests" to search for treatment for my sister, Mary's, hearing problem. That brought back memories of my also "tagging along " with Mom and Dad on a vacation to visit some of my dad's first and second cousins. They lived in Oklahoma. I don't recall if Mary was along or if she was at school in Columbus.

When my dad was in his late teens or early twenties, he had once ridden a motorcycle to Oklahoma to visit these same relatives and to seek his fortune in the booming oil fields. Needless to say, he didn't find a fortune, and before long he returned to Lima. His adventures out there in the early nineteen hundreds, his return home, and his courtship of the fair Faye Showalter will be material for another memoir later on.

Anyway, the year of our family trip was 1935 and the cost of a new four-door Plymouth Belvedere was $565. My dad had done some carpentry work for the C. H. Black, Dodge and Plymouth Agency and he negotiated a deal where he traded in his 1928 Chrysler, along with a sum of cash, for the new Plymouth four-door sedan. I'm sure that Mom insisted on a cash deal, paid in full, as all she wanted to worry about was making that one regular monthly mortgage payment on our house to the South Side Building and Loan.

At any rate, Mom, Dad and I started out for Oklahoma, heading south and west. Of course, this was before the development of our Interstate Highway System of today. What we did have was US Routes. Some of the more famous routes were US 30 (the Lincoln Highway), Route 40 (clear from the East Coast to California) and, of course, the Route made famous by the song, "Get your kicks on Route 66!"

Back then, we didn't have such things as motels; we had "tourist cabins". I think we got about as far as Memphis on our second night, and we settled into a tourist cabin on the east side of the Mississippi River. Of course there were no radios in the cabins, and television was not yet available, so after we got back from supper at a nearby restaurant, we just retired for the evening so we could get an early start in the morning. I'm sure I was tired from all the excitement of the trip, and fell into a deep sleep.

But around two or three in the morning I suddenly felt a terrible pain and a loud noise in my left ear! I woke up screaming and roused my parents, who put on the only light, a bare bulb hanging from a ceiling fixture. Mom asked me what was wrong and, between sobs, I told her I didn't know, but that it would be quiet for a moment and then the noise would start and the pain with it again!

Mom looked in my outer ear but, of course, could not see anything, so she asked Dad to bring in the flashlight from the glove box in the car. He brought it in and handed it to her. She shined the light into my ear, and said she still couldn't see anything. Then the noise started again and, as Mom continued to shine the light, a large, black hard-shelled beetle climbed out, and the pain stopped. Mom shrieked and knocked the beetle off my cheek onto the linoleum floor and smashed it with her shoe!

So, we had learned how to get a beetle out of your ear: just shine a light in there and the beetle will come out to the light.

Needless to say, I didn't get much sleep the rest of the night and Mom tore a hankie into strips (Kleenex hadn't been invented) and plugged both my ears and, I think, hers too,

The next morning, we crossed the Mississippi into Arkansas and found a roadside restaurant to get breakfast. As we came out after eating, I looked over into the field by the place where we had parked our car. It was a cotton field, ready to be harvested and picked. I ran over and got a double-handful of cotton bolls and brought them to the car. I picked the cotton seeds out and, from then on, for the rest of our vacation, I went to bed at night with fresh cotton stuffed into both ears. Never again would I give a beetle or any other insect free access to those areas!

We continued traveling toward our destinations of Norman and Tulsa, Oklahoma. At lunch the next day, after my introduction to "The Beetles," I made another discovery -- "Dr. Pepper"! -- it was never marketed East of the Mississippi until after WWII. Mom let me order it for breakfast, lunch and supper, and I have had a romance with it ever since.

I also started something else on that trip that has stayed with me. I knew that times were hard and we were on a budget so, although Mom or Dad never directed me to, I started automatically looking at the bottom of the menu selections because that is where the cheaper entrees were listed.

Besides, a hamburger or hot dog and a Dr. Pepper was all I needed for *any* meal!

We finally arrived in Norman, Oklahoma to a warm welcome from all of Dad's cousins. I really don't remember too much about the people we visited, and I don't recall any kids my age.

But I do remember that one of my Dad's cousins was establishing a company to market janitorial supplies. He had formulated a compound to sprinkle on the oiled, wooden floors at schools, offices and so forth. When you swept it up, the floors would be clean. I believe he became somewhat successful and did indeed establish a janitorial supply company.

After four or five days, it was time for us to head back to Ohio. I continued to order Dr. Pepper with each meal until we crossed the Mississippi, and then my supply was cut off and I went into acute Dr. Pepper withdrawal symptoms. But, I gradually recovered.

The one big thing I learned from our travels was that I never took a trip thereafter without a big wad of cotton in my Dopp Kit and a small flashlight. I'd had enough "Beetlemania" for the rest of my life.

6. Two Doors East and Two Doors West

When I was growing up, we used to refer to two of our sets of neighbors as "Two Doors East" and "Two Doors West." These two families got a lot of our attention because we were on the same telephone party line. We were all on the Rice exchange and *our* number was Rice-1393. (I think the Rice exchange was named for Rice Avenue, which was two blocks south of us).

Both Mrs. Creviston (two doors east) and Mrs. Hutchinson (two doors west) used the phone a lot. Often when we would pick up the receiver, one of the two would be on the line. Back then, we kids were admonished not to spend much time on the phone. We could usually hear the clicks when neighbors would pick up and listen in. So it was always a temptation to try to ease the receiver off very gently and eavesdrop, ourselves. My mom took a dim view of this -- unless she wanted to listen in.

"Two Doors West" was the Hutchinson family composed of Dr. Hutchinson, a B&O Railroad Doctor, and Mrs. Hutchinson, plus one grown son, Kenneth, who, I think, was in medical school. He was away, at any rate, and I don't recall ever meeting him. I think Fred was Dr. Hutchinson's name but we always referred to him as Doc Hutchinson (but as Doctor Hutchinson in front of Mrs. H.).

Between us and the Hutchinsons was Mr. and Mrs. Frank Speidel. Frank was a railroad engineer on the Pennsy. They lived there till I was about 12 or 14 and then they sold their house to a Mr. and Mrs. Hubert Warner. Hubert was an Allen County Agricultural extension agent.

I don't remember Mrs. Hutchinson's first name. In person I always referred to her as Mrs. Hutchinson but at home to Mom I would call her Mrs. Hutch. She was a tall, attractive lady with an engaging smile, who wore her beautifully coifed gray hair in an upsweep style. She stood erect and had a pleasant, soft eastern accent. I don't know if it is a proper term, but as a boy, I would have called her a very handsome lady.

She was extremely frightened of dogs and even of our little beagle, Queenie, who was a friend to everyone, even the hobos who came to ask for a handout. If Queenie would walk into the living room where Mrs. Hutchinson and Mom were having coffee, we would see a "flying saucer" and a cup in the air. Needless to say, we tried to keep Old Queen away from Mrs. Hutch and from the property Two Doors West.

Mrs. Hutchinson had a railroad pass because of her husband's work and used it a great deal to travel back to New York and environs, and sometimes to Chicago. Whenever she would be gone for a while, she would always call Mom on her return (She never talked to our neighbors One Door West, because the man of the house was an engineer on the Pennsy, a rival company). Mom would always volunteer my services for needed tasks and supply errands. My bike had a basket on the front and I could easily fetch things from Johnson's Grocery at the corner of Jameson and Delphos Road.

Mrs. Hutchinson micromanaged me and would correct my language and appearance when Mom wasn't around. I didn't mind in the least, though, because of her gentility and her musical voice and laugh. One time when she offered me fifty cents for running some errands for her, I attempted to refuse it, and got a lecture that when someone offers you something, you must have the grace to accept it and not refuse it. They want you to have it or they wouldn't offer, she said, so from then on, I was anxious to run any errand she wanted. I suppose her generosity was a carryover from the tipping for services in New York.

Well, one day Dr. Hutchinson got transferred to Cleveland or New York or some place, and we were no longer to see Mrs. Hutch any more. We missed her grand visage walking up Hazel Avenue, impeccably dressed and coiffed, and often wearing a mink scarf or jacket. What a gal!

Two Doors East lived the Crevistons: Earl, Ruth, son Bob, and daughter Lavina Ruth. Earl was alternately in the lumber and hardware business. Ruth was a dainty little lady and walked, you may remember, with a pronounced limp because polio had affected her right leg. She was a bright lady and had graduated from Ohio Wesleyan. She talked on the phone a lot to her mother who lived on Brice Avenue near Metcalf. Ruth's father, a Rev. Helms, was a Methodist minister who later went up the clerical ladder to become a Methodist Bishop.

Because of her leg, Ruth couldn't drive and depended on her mother for many errands such as grocery shopping. I don't think the Crevistons even

29

really had a car, as they didn't have a garage and I never saw a car in their driveway.

Bob Creviston was only six months older than me, but Ruth got him into school a year earlier, which Bob always regretted. Bob was a very good student and a masterful piano player.

Lavina Ruth was considered a slow student and went to special ed classes at Horace Mann. However, I would classify her as anything but slow as she became a voracious reader and had a pleasant personality despite all. When not in school, she spent a great deal of time at the dining room window, peering out from behind the curtain onto Hazel Avenue. She kept her mom posted on everything that went on out on the street. We had a standing joke that when we went past Two Doors East, we could see the curtains part and we knew that Lavina was "tending curtain."

Ruth was a godsend to me when it came time to plan my high school curriculum because my folks didn't really know how to direct me. Agreeing with the plans voiced for me by my brother, Marvin, who was ten years my senior, Ruth put me into the college prep course: physics, chemistry, German, and the whole nine yards. After graduation, she and my brother urged me to enroll in college and get started, despite the war, until such time as I might get called for military service.

Later on, when I opened my office to practice medicine, Ruth and Lavina Ruth became my patients. Ruth had learned to drive and became, first, a substitute teacher and then, when the school allowed full-time teachers to be married, she became a full-time teacher.

Earl had moved them to a small village where they operated a little hardware store together. But when Earl's illness polished him off, Ruth returned to full-time teaching to support herself and Lavina. She had to drive thirty miles to school every day in all kinds of weather -- snowstorms and rain -- and then drive back home.

Her right hip was deteriorated and was giving her fits and this was in the days before hip replacements. She came to see me and I sat her down and it was my turn to lecture to her. I advised her to get out of this vile weather and move to Florida and, eventually, she and Lavina settled in Bradenton. Several times, when our family was driving to Miami to visit relatives, we stopped in Bradenton to see them. They were doing great and were thankful they had made the move.

As Ruth's infirmities worsened, she was able to get both herself and Lavina into a life-time care, church-oriented home in Bradenton, similar to Shell Point Village where Polly and I live.

Ruth died in about 1993, but she had made arrangements for Lavina to stay on in their condo. Lavina has since moved into an assisted living facility and sent us a Christmas card last year.

- - -

This ends the saga of Two Doors East and Two Doors West. From one, I learned to think and plan ahead and, from the other, I learned how to graciously accept a compliment or a reward for my services.

Grade School Years

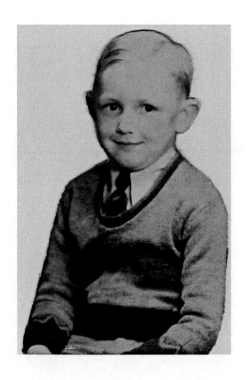

7. My Most Memorable Grade School Teacher

From 1931 to 1937, I attended the Horace Mann elementary school which was only a block and a half from where I lived. In those days, there were no school cafeterias and we all went home at noon for lunch. We also had no kindergarten, which came along later, so we started school right in the first grade.

My first grade teacher was Miss Hathaway. She taught us all to fold our hands on our desks when we were finished with a task. One day, I had finished a little ahead of the rest of the class and was sitting with my hands folded, humming.

Thinking she would embarrass me and stop me from humming, she asked me if I would like to get up in front of the class and sing a song. I said "Sure!" and I marched up to the front of the class and began to sing "Jesus Loves Me." As soon as I was finished, she ushered me back to my seat and said that there would be no more humming.

My second grade teacher, Miss Colucci, was quite stern, and I was glad to get out of the second grade. Lo and behold, on the first day of the third grade, who walks into the room but Miss Colucci, who had been promoted with us to the third grade!

My fourth grade teacher, Miss Edstrand, went to my church and was also my Sunday school teacher, so we got along pretty well.

My fifth grade teacher, Miss Williams, lived far out in Allen County in a Welsh settlement. It was always difficult for her to get to school in the winter time because of the deep snows we used to have. This may partly explain why she always smelled like Vick's Vaporub and Hall's mentholyptus cough drops, and she always seemed to have a cold and a cough, from September to April.

Now, the sixth grade teacher, Miss Van Cleve, was something else. She was the principal and she meted out the discipline for all six grades. She was from Oklahoma and was not about to put up with any tomfoolery. She was a female version of Gen. George S. Patton ten years before his time.

When school would get out at noon, and at the end of the day, there was no hurry-scurry noisy leaving of the building. General Van Cleve had us all line up in rows four-abreast and march out the front door where she surveyed the troops, while Miss Edstrand played stirring John Philip Sousa marches on the piano in the hall.

One day at noon, I was doing a high-stepping march when suddenly I was jerked out of formation and found myself looking up into the dreaded icy blue eyes of General Van Cleve. She took me back to the little kitchen where she kept her paddle. She gave me a couple of swats on the rear end and asked me if I thought I would remember how to march from then on. She didn't have to tell me twice.

In Miss Van Cleve's classroom, she had written the rules of grammar and the definition of terms in beautiful script along the top of the blackboard, all around the room. Woe unto anyone who accidentally erased any portion thereof!

She was a stickler for paying attention in class. One day, we were reading in our *Weekly Reader* newspaper and she called on me and I had been wool gathering and had lost the place. . .

Another trip to the kitchen!

However, I must admit that her discipline really ingrained her messages and teaching. Seven years later, when I was taking the Proficiency Entrance Exams at college, I could close my eyes and see her rules of grammar at the top of the board and the answers came so easily to me, I almost felt as though I was cheating.

Miss Van Cleve was indeed one of the finest teachers I have ever had.

8. A Saturday Night in Lima, 1930's Style

Being retired in Florida nowadays, I don't yet have established connections for good historical information such as folks in Lima can get at the Historical Society or the library. But I do remember a lot about Lima in the 30s and would like to tell you about some of it. If I have made any errors of date or place, I humbly beg your pardon.

Back in the early 1930's, Lima and Allen County were slowly working their way up and out of the Depression.

The WPA (the Federal relief program, Works Progress Administration) was established and running there, and was the primary source of laborers for the Lima Stadium, which was being built at the time. Green and Sawyer was the contractor and my dad was the foreman on the job.

Folks were cautious with what little money they had and would seek entertainment and recreation that didn't cost much, if anything.

On Saturday mornings, kids would either walk into downtown Lima or ride the streetcar to Main Street. That was where the Lyric, the Rialto, and the Sigma Theaters were. Farther out on South Main was the Majestic.

On Saturday mornings, these theaters would all vie for the young customers. For your admission price, you would get one good cowboy show, an episode from a serial (to keep you coming back each week), a newsreel, and a cartoon. The main show might star Hopalong Cassidy, Tom Mix, Hoot Gibson or various other cowboys. (The singing cowboys, Gene Autry and Roy Rogers and Dale Evans, came along a little later.) For the sum total of a quarter, you could buy carfare to and from the area, a movie admission, and a box of popcorn or a Sugar Daddy.

Man, we were wading in high cotton!

Later in the afternoon and towards evening, the adults would begin filtering in downtown. Some men had to work six days a week, which included Saturday, and they and their families would be the late arrivals. People would begin jockeying for prime parking spots up and down Main Street and in the Square.

The people-watching was about to start. . .

Saturday night in Lima was like a big Block Party, before the term was born. People would sit in their cars with their windows down and greet acquaintances in the passing parade. The aroma of caramel corn from Dome's Nut Shop wafted over the whole downtown area, beckoning the customers who stood in line.

Over in the Square, the Ark of Sweets soda fountain would be busy, as would be the soda fountain in the Woolworth's Five and Dime store. The Equity Dairy sold a unique ice cream scoop that was a slender cone of ice cream that would be set on a sugar cone base.

My folks' favorite parking spot was either on North Main in front of Feldman's Department Store or down on East High just below Walgreen's.

One of the things I remember about downtown Lima is the two public restrooms on the northwest corner of North Street and Main, by the Courthouse.

39

These restrooms were, to my young mind, the nicest and cleanest public facilities I had ever seen.

You entered the Men's restroom off the sidewalk on North Street by a down staircase to a basement level. It had white porcelain tiling and polished fixtures, kept very tidy. I can't speak for the Ladies restroom, but I assume it was just as nice. The Ladies Room entry was on Main Street and it was subterranean also. Those restrooms were oases, and I don't recall any graffiti or other despoiling of the walls or fixtures. As often happens with public facilities, these become misused over time, and the restrooms were eventually closed and the entrances cemented over in the mid-50's.

People from all walks of life and all the sectors of our economy would come to town on Saturday night. My folks were each raised on a farm and so they would see and greet many of their farm friends.

The stores were all open, and business flourished. My folks did a great deal of their shopping at Wright's Market on the corner of High and Union, across from the Barr Hotel. When you entered, you could smell the dill pickle barrel and the barrel with the smoked herring or "Blind Robin." Nearby were the cheeses, with Limburger leading the aroma barrage.

These food stores had no grocery carts to push around. To get items from your list, you would hail a clerk and start telling him what you wanted. You would tell him your first item, he would go and get it, and then you'd tell your next item, etc. It was a very inefficient method, but each housewife felt as if she were being "personally served."

If a list were too long, the clerks got smart and would ask for Madame's list, and then they would quickly gather everything and place it on the counter. Then they would add up the cost of the items on a brown paper sack. After you paid your bill, they would bag your groceries for you and make sure that you got the sack with the figures on it for your receipt. Then you would tote your purchases off to your car.

I guess I was a typically observant youngster at five years of age. One night, we saw a blind man with a white cane standing against a storefront on East High. He was wearing a cap and had a cup in his hand. He would sing softly and occasionally a passerby would put a coin in his cup. He would thank them and deftly pour the coin into his other hand and pocket it.

On a subsequent Saturday, my folks and I parked on East High. When my folks started heading for Wright's Market, I asked them if I could stay in the car and Mom said yes. I had smuggled a tin cup into the backseat when we left home . . .

When I saw my folks disappear into Wright's, I got out of the car and pulled my ball cap down, backed up to a dark storefront, held out my cup and began to sing.

Every once in a while, I would open one eye and look into the cup but, alas, no coins were there. So I would close my eyes and begin again. I guess I was singing "Jesus Wants Me for a Sunbeam" because I didn't know too many other songs at age five. Well, that went on for a while, when -- *WHOOSH!* -- all of a sudden, my feet left the sidewalk, the rear door to our car was opened, and I was summarily deposited therein.

41

I heard my Mom say brusquely, "Start the car, Emmett! Let's go!" I could hear my Dad chuckling as he backed out of the parking place, and off we went. I don't recall that I got to go back to Wright's with Mom for a long time.

They must have missed me over there, though, because they closed that store and moved out onto Spencerville Road and became Wright's IGA Foodliner, complete with grocery carts, as though to attract me back.

And that, incidentally, was about when the whole downtown started to fold.

(Speaking of folding, we used to have a restaurant called Jack and Yoshi's and, later, Jack's Cafeteria, run by two immigrants from Japan. I don't recall, exactly, but I think Jack and Yoshi's closed not too long after Pearl Harbor. Jack's Cafeteria, where I first tasted chop suey and chow mein, kept going after Jack and Yoshi's closed, and was across the street from the old High Street Market, which was a cosmos of its own.)

All in all, we had quite a nice downtown. We had Gregg's Department Store, Feldman's Department Store, The Leader Store, and the Bluem's Store, in addition to J.C. Penney's, Sears and Roebuck, Montgomery Wards and the Blattner's store.

So, as I say, Saturday night in Lima was like a Block Party before there was such a thing, and I think Jesus still wants me for a sunbeam even if I did make Mom angry.

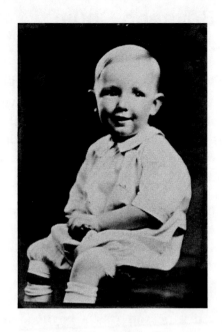

*Age 5, when I
basically knew
one song . . .*

9. What I Learned from a Boyhood Chum

As we make our way through life, some person or some experience will frequently leave footprints on the beaches of our memories. Oftentimes, these footprints are washed away by the tides of time, but sometimes not completely. Some remain imprinted in our memories.

These may not be footprints of a celebrity, or a teacher, or an "important" person, or those of a great historical or monumental experience. Sometimes, they are just the impressions left by a person we considered a friend or even just an acquaintance at the time.

Such a person was a boyhood friend of mine, who was a second-grader when I first met him and he began walking on the beaches of my memory. In the interests of his privacy and that of any others, I will call him "Eldon."

Eldon lived about three blocks west of me on Hazel Avenue, in a neighborhood that had predated my neighborhood by twenty or thirty years. Although the homes in that area were older, and some were a little dilapidated, most were fairly well-maintained.

Eldon lived in a one-floor home with his mother, father, and younger sister, Betty. Eldon's father was a coal hauler for the Lima Ice and Coal Company.

I first met Eldon as he walked past my house on his way to the Horace Mann Elementary School. I began walking with him to and from school, twice a day, because we went home for our lunch.

About two blocks west of Eldon's house, Hazel Avenue dead-ended into a large woods owned by a Mr. Baxter. As we would walk and talk, Eldon told me of some of his expeditions and explorations into the woods. He soon had my curiosity up and got my eagerness to share his adventure to a fevered pitch.

One Fall day, he asked me if I would like to go hickory nut hunting with him after school and I eagerly responded that I'd love to go! We stopped at my house where I introduced Eldon to my mom and told her what we planned to do.

I got her permission to go and, while I changed into my exploring and nut-hunting clothes, Mom talked with Eldon and told him that she knew his father because he would occasionally deliver coal to our house. Mom gave me a cloth, ten-pound sugar sack to store my booty and treasures.

We next went to Eldon's house and I met his mother and waited on the front porch while he changed clothes.

At this point, I must tell you that Eldon wore round, black horn-rimmed glasses, and looked just like the Harry Potter of today -- this was 65 years ago. Not only that, but his mom wore identical black horn-rimmed glasses, and looked like what I would imagine Harry Potter's mom might.

Well, off we went to Baxter's Woods. We climbed the gate and entered our enchanted forest. As we went along, Eldon pointed out the various trees: hickory, walnut, beech, oak, birch and horse chestnut. We had great nut hunting and filled our sacks with nice hulled hickory nuts, being careful to discard the ones with worm holes.

This day was just the first of our many forays into the wonderland of Baxter's Woods. In addition to the nuts, we found bittersweet to take home to our moms.

In the winter, Eldon told me to bring my sled and we went deep into the woods and came to an area near the Pennsylvania Railroad. There was a large culvert there and a nice sliding hill with a pond at the bottom. There was also a hobo's camp where we would build a fire and roast potatoes in foil while we sledded.

I never saw Eldon much in the summer, being busy with the boys in my neighborhood, playing baseball, roller skating and all the many things that keep grade school boys occupied. When the school year resumed in the fall, Eldon would start walking by, and our friendship would take up where it had left off in the spring.

Once, in the 4th grade, Eldon didn't come by for a couple of days, so I walked down to his house to see him. I froze in my tracks when I saw a "Black Wreath" by the front door. Back then, when someone passed away, their body lay in state in the living room or parlor for the friends and relatives to pay their respects. The black wreath announced the wake.

Eldon's mom had had cancer, and had died, and Eldon had never said anything about it to me at all.

Needless to say, my chum was markedly depressed, and we would walk to school in silence. He never cried or said much, but I guess it helped to just have someone with whom to walk.

In January, when the snows began to be heavy, Eldon and I formed a partnership to shovel snow from people's walks. I would knock on the door, while Eldon would begin shoveling, and I would negotiate a price. Then we would clean the walks and split the fee.

Oft times, we would go to a grocery store or a bakery after we had finished shoveling for the day and reward ourselves. I noticed that Eldon would frequently spend everything he had earned.

I asked him once why he didn't save some for a rainy day. It was then that he told me that his dad most often came home drunk, and if Eldon had any money, his dad would take it from him and buy himself more beer with it. So, Eldon would spend it all beforehand.

Later, Eldon built himself a tree house beside his garage. Then he would keep his money in a tobacco can in the tree house because his dad wouldn't climb up there.

Our friendship flourished throughout the grade school years, but when we got to high school, we were on different tracks. He was in the General Studies Course and I was in the College Prep course that my older brother had outlined for me. I gradually lost

47

track of Eldon and don't remember seeing him after graduation.

When I was preparing to write this story, I called a friend who is our class historian and asked if he knew about Eldon. He said he could vaguely remember him and said he would search his yearbooks and get back to me. I had told him about the glasses and when he called me back, he said that Harry Potter had jumped right off the page at him in a picture from the 1943 yearbook.

He said that Eldon had joined the Navy (which may have been his way out of the house) and became an electrician's mate, moved to Illinois, married and had six children. He was reported deceased at our 25th class reunion, which would have made him about 43 or 44 years old.

I would guess that he was a good father to his six kids and tried to provide, as so many of us have wished to do, something better than he had experienced himself as a kid.

And so, as I said in the beginning, sometimes the footprints of memory are not washed away by the tides of time. The recent pictures of Harry Potter that have been popular have jogged my memory and reminded me of a chum who taught me many things.

From Eldon, I learned how to identify the hickory, walnut, beech, maple, and oak trees in Baxter's Woods.

And from Eldon, I learned that life is not always fair. It is not fair for a ten year old boy to lose his mother and be forced to endure harsh circumstances at home. I learned that not every kid is as lucky as I was to have a mom and dad and brothers and a sister who loved me. This was more effective than reading about it in a social studies book.

And lastly, I learned that, sometimes, it helps just to walk with your friend in silence.

10. "Someday, I'll Live There"

Growing up in Lima was a wonderful experience, but it did have a few drawbacks for an eight year old boy. The land is pretty flat and the only good sledding hills were more than a mile from our house.

To go sledding, I had to walk a block to the 1000 block of North Cole Street, and then fourteen blocks south. I would cross over Market Street, the dividing road between North and South, and end up in Faurot Park. Each city block was 1/10th of a mile, so that meant my journey was approximately a mile-and-a-half.

As I passed the houses on the 400 block of South Cole Street and crossed over Lakewood Avenue, I would be greeted by the old World War I cannon that guarded the entrance to the park. I think that almost every kid who grew up in Lima, at one time or another, played on that cannon and turned the handles, which were loose and unlocked.

On a Saturday in the winter, if conditions were right, I would make the trip from home to the sledding trails in Faurot Park. After stashing my ice skates off my sled in a hiding place, I would begin sledding down the "Big Hill" on my Flexible Flyer.

What a thrill to go flying silently down that icy slope! On one occasion, a boy about my age walked into the narrow tree-lined sledding trail in front of me and it was impossible for me to change my course and although I shouted a warning he didn't hear me . . . .

50

My sled struck him just below the calves of his legs. As he flipped up in the air, I glided underneath and stopped my sled as quickly as I could. Fortunately, like me, he was wearing a pair of leather high-top boots (with the knife pocket on the right boot) and he wasn't hurt -- just surprised -- and he realized that I couldn't help it, so there was no fracas.

When I got tired of sledding, I would go and retrieve my ice skates and head down to the skating pond. Sitting on my sled and taking off my boots, I would next put on those freezing-cold shoe skates.

After a couple of turns around the ice-skating pond, my feet would be warmed up, and I would join a group of skaters playing "crack the whip." All newcomers had to take the end position and be cracked and rifled across the ice when the "conga" line suddenly turned and snapped. We weren't too popular with the serious skaters.

When the onset of evening was imminent, I would go over to the pond-side bonfire that was always kept lit during winter sports, and which would by then be dying down, and take off my ice skates and put on my icy high-top boots, lacing the frozen laces with numb fingers. Then I would put my wet gloves back on, pull my frozen pant legs down over my boots, put my ice skates on my sled, and begin the trek home.

As I passed those big brick and stucco homes with their warm, cheery, lighted windows, I promised myself that "Some day, I would live on South Cole Street, near the park."

How good it was to turn off North Cole Street onto Hazel Avenue, go in the side door at 1158, and take off my wet gloves, frozen pants, and wet socks. Then Mom would always say, "It's a good thing you are home. I was just about to come after you if I'd have known where to find you."

- - -

Well, in 1958, it happened. . .

My dad, the builder who had constructed my office, had said that he would like to build me a house, but by the time I thought I could afford a mortgage and a new house, he was in his late 70's and didn't think he could take on such a big project.

He suggested that Polly and I find an older home that we liked and that he would remodel it to our taste. In June of 1958, twenty-five years after my park escapades, we signed the papers to purchase 424 South Cole Street. Dad put new Andersen windows in the front sun room, paneled the living room with beautiful cherry paneling, and remodeled the kitchen, putting in an island and a breakfast nook.

Upstairs, he put new Andersen windows in a sun/bed room and remodeled a bathroom. Our kids were six, four-and-a-half and three years old when we moved in, and our last daughter was born in October of that year. The kids all got to sled, ice skate, and toboggan in Faurot Park and they only had to walk a block!

I finally "lived there"!

11. Horace Mann Grade School, Revisited

Several things happened in the spring and summer of 2002 that have made me want to revisit my grade school in story form.

In May of this year, my wife, Polly, and I attended "The Patriotic Pops" at the Naples Philharmonic, conducted by Erich Kunzel. Besides the local orchestra, the concert featured the U. S. Army Chorus and also the 114-member Philharmonic Youth Chorale. I think it was all those charming children, grades 1 through 9, on stage with the Soldiers Chorus and the orchestra, that made me recall the many musical events, folk dances, and departures from the 3 R's that we had at school.

This past summer, our youngest daughter visited our hometown of Lima and brought me back some wonderful pictures showing how Horace Mann school looked when I was there from 1931 to 1937. It was really a step back in time. . .

Old Horace Mann was a foreboding brick facade, complete with a belfry and wrought iron fire escapes all around the building. It had been a Lutheran college, known as the Lima College, until the city school system bought it in 1908. During 1932-1933, labor forces from the WPA removed the belfry and the third floor.

All up and down Jameson Avenue, where the school stood, were big, beautiful, old homes that had belonged to the professors and officials of the college I remember one spectacular house, about two lots from Hazel Avenue on the east side of Jameson, which had a huge third floor promontory. The owner used to keep homing pigeons in the loft. He would let the pigeons out in the evenings to exercise and they would fly over, around, and into, the belfry of the college. At twilight, they would all return to the loft.

When I entered Horace Mann School, I naturally learned the basics. But my most vivid memories are of the artistic and creative activities we enjoyed. I would like to tell you about these. Not too much in these areas happened during my first three years of school. Basically, we just smeared a lot of library paste around. It wasn't until the fourth grade, in Miss Edstrand's class, that we began having Miss Violet Lewis come on Tuesday afternoons to introduce us to music.

Then on Friday afternoons, we would have art, and my favorite art teacher was Miss Lela Klinger. She always wore such bright and pretty colors -- reds, greens, yellows, oranges and purples -- in a very pleasing manner. (Sometimes, Miss Mary Kirk would substitute, but she wore darker and, to my eye, somewhat duller clothes.)

Miss Edstrand and the other fourth grade teacher, Miss Mary Tullis, began introducing us to folk dancing, as well as to folk songs and ballads. We would always have to perform our latest folk dances and songs for the PTA ladies meeting on the last Friday afternoon of the month.

In 1936, the Welsh community near Gomer, named Vaughnsville, along with the northwest part of

Allen County, planned an *Eisteddfod*. An *Eisteddfod* is an annual meeting of Welsh poets and minstrels, a movable feast that was usually held in a different place each year, and it would last several days. It consisted of readings, all forms of vocal music--including solos, quartets and choruses -- and, of course, folk dancing.

I had never heard of an *Eisteddfod*, let alone seen one, but it was announced one day that our two fifth grades at Horace Mann had been invited to perform at an *Eisteddfod*, to be held in Lima Memorial Hall later on that spring. (Could it be that Miss Williams, our teacher, who was Welsh and lived in Gomer, had something to do with our invitation?)

Feverish preparations and planning thereupon began. It was decided that the boys in the two fifth-grade classes would be combined into one group and be dressed in bellbottom pants, white shirts and white sailor's caps, and would sing and dance the Sailor's Hornpipe. I would be less than honest if I failed to confess that the Hornpipe number ended up being one of the favorite performances of the whole Eisteddfod.

In the Fall, the art teachers would have us make paper leaves and pumpkin faces. On Friday of that week, or on Halloween, you could wear a Halloween costume in the afternoon if you wished. Then we would have donuts and cider. *Whoopee*!

One event that would break up the humdrum of winter was in February, Valentine's Day! For a couple of weeks before February 14th, our art class would construct a big box to put valentines in to be taken out and delivered to the recipients later during a party. We could either make the valentines or buy them. It was suggested that if you put any valentines in the box, you should have one for each class member. However, if you had a crush on someone, you might buy a special valentine that contained a lollipop inside.

Towards the end of April, when things were getting dull, we would prepare for the May Day Celebration on May 1st. Our playground tetherball pole was transformed into a beautiful May Pole for the festivities, with long ribbons in all colors that reached from the top to the ground. This celebration was primarily for the sixth graders and was, in effect, a farewell to their grade school days.

A large circle of students, alternating boys and girls, would surround the pole and each one would take a streamer of ribbon and, as the music played (usually on a wind-up Victrola), the girls would walk in one direction and the boys in the opposite direction, moving in and out of each other so as to weave a beautiful May Pole. When the pole was finished, the Queen of the May, whom the students had previously chosen, was crowned.

The May Day rites go back a long way. I once read a line in one of Tennyson's poems that said, "For I am to be Queen of the May, Mother."

Well, the grade school days passed . . .

When we graduated to Junior High, I still had some contact with Miss Klinger and Miss Kirk in Art class. But music instruction had become more choral, and also more formal in nature. For some reason or other, I was never invited to participate in the choruses.

Oh, well--that was their loss. In our church choir, I was a boy soprano and sang solo renditions of Handel's "I Know That My Redeemer Liveth," and "He Leadeth Me," so I know I had to be okay!

Long afterwards, my school day memories were unexpectedly stirred in a poignant way - - -

Years later, I had become the medical director for Shawnee Manor Nursing Home, a large facility, and -- lo and behold! -- who was I to find one day as a new patient assigned to me but my colorful Miss Klinger! She was quite crippled with arthritis by then and seemed somewhat depressed. She brightened up when I recalled our prior encounters as student and teacher thirty or so years before.

I made it a requisite to see her each time I went to the nursing home rather than to make just a monthly visit. I asked her what I could do to improve things for her. She smiled and said she would like to have a glass of port wine before dinner each night, but she doubted if that would be possible.

I took leave of her, and returned in a half-hour with a bottle of port. I took it to the nursing desk and wrote an order on her chart, saying that Miss Klinger was to have 3 ounces of port 30 minutes before her evening meal, and that, when the bottle ran low, I was to be notified so I could replace it. Miss Klinger was most grateful and, happily, her depression seemed to abate.

12. The Day the Circus Came To Town

One of the biggest events of the year when I was growing up was the day the circus came to town. It happened almost every year, and sometimes two or three times a year, as there were several circuses back then.

The biggest and best, of course, was the Ringling Brothers, Barnum and Bailey Three-Ring Circus. The next-best circus, although some would argue that it was the best, was the Hagenbeck and Wallace Circus, which was originally from Hamburg, Germany. Later in my growing up years, several smaller circuses would come to town also, the most notable one being Clyde Beatty's Wild Animal Circus.

Back when I was in grade school, the circuses all traveled by railroad. Lima was a favorite site for the circuses because of the five railroads passing through. We had great stretches of rail sidings where the circus trains would unload, park for a time, and then load up for the trip to the next show site.

The advance men for the circus would hit town several weeks before the appointed circus days. Sometimes, a circus would play for two or even three days if the market was good. Signs would go up on the telephone poles and in the storefronts -- big, beautiful, multi-colored cardboard signs that made every kid salivate with excitement and anticipation.

Sometimes the advance men would make some kind of a deal with the school system and, if a kid

59

bought a ticket for the Friday afternoon matinee show, he or she could get out of school to attend the performance. I was usually able to coax Mom to take several kids in my class and me to the Big Show in our 1928 Chrysler. Sometimes, on the first school day after the circus, those who had gone to it had to give oral reports to the rest of the class about what they had seen at the circus.

On the morning the circus came into town, if it came in from the west, from Ft. Wayne on the Pennsy, I would be in luck. Mom would wake me up at about six AM and hurry me to get dressed and eat breakfast. Then she and I would start walking east on Hazel Avenue to College Avenue and about two-and-a-half blocks to Delphos Road. There before my eyes was a magnificent sight: the circus train unloading!

It was like a Cecile B. DeMille movie set, as crowds of people would come to watch the spectacle. There were elephants pushing wagons with their heads. There were beautiful horses pulling cages on wheels with lions and tigers inside. Circus hands would be leading camels and zebras. Sometimes a small tractor would pull the big steam calliope off the train and then a four- or six-horse team would be hooked to it.

(An interesting side note: Naturally, the animals would have to relieve themselves and many spectators came with shovels and baskets to scoop up the manure for their gardens. After all, how many people could claim to fertilize their gardens with camel or elephant manure? This may not be recommended and sanctioned by Master Gardeners and I don't know

60

if compost piles were in vogue back then. But this was a popular thing to do.)

Sometimes the circus would parade down Main Street on the way to the Vine Street show grounds or to those on East Kibby Street. There the steam calliope and the circus brass band would put on a great musical entertainment show, thereby enticing more people to come out to the circus.

I never really got to see them set up the tents, but I'm told that the workers used the horses and elephants to pull the poles into position. Then the roustabouts would start driving stakes, and ropes would appear from the tops of the poles, and all of a sudden -- *"Presto!"* -- the Big Top would be up. Next, the sideshow tents would go up, to house "The Fat Lady," "Jo-Jo, the Dog-Faced Boy," the snake charmer, and so on.

We would leave home for the circus at least an hour-and-a-half before show time, park as close as we could, and then walk to the main entrance, give them our tickets, and then be inside the circus grounds. We'd spend some of our hard-earned money on cotton candy, saltwater taffy, and circus peanuts to eat while we watched the show. We would walk past the sideshows and look at the garish signs about those within. But, we were never allowed to go inside the sideshows.

Finally, we would enter the Big Top that housed the Three Rings. I don't recall that there were any reserved seats, so we would rush to get the best seats we could find, and position ourselves in our space, getting ready to watch "The Greatest Show On Earth."

The Ringmaster would come in on a beautiful white horse and direct our attention to the first ring, where fancy-dressed girls would be standing on the backs of galloping horses. In the middle ring, there would be elephants going in a circle, with each one holding the tail of the one ahead using his trunk.

Then there would be the clowns, and the lion tamer in the cage with the big cats, cracking his whip and putting them through their paces. Our attention would be called to the far ring where a big cannon was located. A man would slide feet-first down the barrel and then --*BOOM!* --he'd be shot into a net!

Nearing the finale, the ringmaster would direct us to the trapeze artists who were performing their breath-taking leaps and tumbles, and then we would hear the familiar song:

"Once I was happy, but now I'm forlorn,
Like an old coat that is tattered and torn,
Left in this wide world to weep and to mourn,
Betrayed by a maid in her teens!

"The girl that I loved, she was handsome
And I tried all I knew, her to please.
But I never could please her one-quarter so well
As the man on the flying trapeze!

"He flies through the air with the greatest of ease,
The daring young man on the flying trapeze.
His movements were graceful,
    all the girls he would please,
And my love he has purloined away!"

So, that usually ended the show, and as soon as they could clear all the spectators out of the circus grounds, the tents began to come down and the bleachers were disassembled. Everything was packed and folded away, and the trek back to the train on the siding began.

I never actually saw the trains load up again and depart, but I imagine it was another Cecile B. DeMille movie set all over again. I've been told that the roustabouts slept underneath the wagons on the floors of the railroad cars. That seems like a poor way to treat such hard-working men. Maybe that is why I never wanted to run away and join the circus.

Soon the posters were taken off the telephone poles and out of the storefronts, and, within a few days, when we would go down Delphos Avenue beside the rail siding, the Master Gardeners had cleaned up all the elephant and camel manure and you couldn't tell any more that "The Greatest Show On Earth" had ever been there.

Then all we could do was remember The Greatest Show, and wait for its return next year . . .

13. The Playground at Horace Mann School

Every summer, a week or two after the school year ended at Horace Mann grade school, we would have Vacation Bible School at Calvary Evangelical and Reformed Church on Richie Avenue. Bible School would last for two weeks. After that, it was time for me to pick cherries and begin the endless grass mowing, spring cleaning, rug-beating, cleaning of the lily pond and weeding of the rock garden that would occupy me for much of the season.

But around the end of June or first of July, when our Bible School was over, the Horace Mann Summer playground would open for business!

There were four clay tennis courts there that were off-limits to all playground kids. The teenage cousins of Bob Creviston supervised the area. These kids -- Clara Jean, Ray, and Jim -- were older than most of my friends. They hosed down the courts, raked and brushed them, and applied the court lines with lime. They controlled the reservations and collected all the fees. If someone wanted to play singles, it would cost each player fifty cents, or a total of a dollar an hour. If it was doubles, each player would pay twenty-five cents an hour, for a dollar total. That was a lot of money back in 1933!

On the playgrounds nearby was a large, square equipment shed, which was kept locked. But when the director would come at 9 AM to open the playground.

the big door of the shed would be swung open, revealing all the treasures within.

There was a pleasant, musty, dusty leather smell in the shack. On the inside of the doors would be posted calendars and schedules of events planned. There were shelves with equipment, and there were chests with bats, softballs and ball gloves in them. You would also see tennis balls and the nets and paddles for the paddle tennis courts. (Since the clay tennis courts were off-limits to us kids, we were placated with "paddle tennis".)

There were also volleyball nets, volleyballs, croquet mallets, wickets, and croquet balls. And there were boxes of chalk for drawing hopscotch courts on the main walk from Jameson to the school's front entrance.

Speaking of the school entrance, the restroom facilities for the playground were always just inside that first door and down the basement. I never saw such dark, dank restrooms in all my life, but they were nonetheless the coolest place around in the hot summer, before the days of air conditioning.

All the permanent fixtures of the playground were of industrial durability. The swing set -- two groups of three swings each -- was made of cast iron frames set in concrete. The iron chains that suspended the swings from the frame had rigid, foot-long links. The wooden seats were each an inch thick. The really hard use of the swings was by high school boys, who would pump hard repeatedly until they were swinging up as high as the top bar. Once they had this kind of forward momentum, they would jump off the seats at the "apogee" point of going horizontal to see how far out in front of the swings they could land.

The teeter-totter was also of industrial grade, with very thick boards and sturdy handles. The usual dirty trick was to let down all your weight so the person on the other end was up at the top, and then to jump off your end of the board and let them come crashing down -- not very nice, and quite dangerous.

We had a "sea wave," low-slung merry-go-round that was leg-powered. Also, there was a huge sandbox that was apparently far enough away from the neighborhood cats so that we never got any "unsavory deposits."

The playground directors would set up tournaments for many games, such as hopscotch, jacks and marbles. There would also be paddle tennis tournaments. The paddle tennis net was just knee-high, and the game was played the same as tennis, except on a smaller court. The players would use a solid wooden paddle that was approximately two or three times the size of a ping-pong paddle.

There would also be hopscotch tournaments, with chalked courts on the front walk, and jacks tournaments. There would be girls' leagues and boys' leagues. The winner of the girls would play the winner of the boys, and the girls always won in both jacks and hopscotch.

Marble tournaments were another of our games. Each boy had his own bag of marbles and he generally had a favorite large "shooter," a big, solid marble. Each kid also usually had a big chrome roller bearing, which he would sometimes use as a shooter. Before each contest, the prudent player would shout "No steelies!" and that meant that no one could use his big roller bearing as an unfair shooter. We didn't need an adult as referee because the kids made the rules as they went. It was forbidden to play marbles "for keeps" during playground hours.

Now, choosing up sides for a softball game was a procedure to behold; today's leaders could take a lesson. A bunch of kids would decide to play softball and the playground director would "bug off" and observe from the perimeter.

The kids would choose two leaders. The two would face each other and one would toss a bat vertically to the other one, who would grab the bat at about the middle. Then the tosser would grab the bat immediately above, and tight against the fist of, the catcher, who would then put his fist grip above his opponent's. Eventually, one of the guys would look at the amount of bat left and, if he felt that the other guy's grip would not fit under the lip of the bat handle, he would shout, "No chicken grips!" This meant that the last guy was not allowed to grasp the end of the bat with just a thumb and a finger or two, like a chicken or hawk, to win the toss.

Well, whoever won the toss would get the first choice of players. Then the loser would get the next choice, and so on, until the teams were chosen. Then the players would all agree on where the bases were, and the out-of-bounds, and on all the necessary rules. This was all done without the playground director's providing a "psychological group learning experience." We did it our way!

Generally, the playground would close at 5 PM. The equipment building was locked, the school was locked and the playground went to sleep. All the kids would leave and go home for supper . . .

But, after supper, those of us who lived just across the street from the playground would return and begin the forbidden game of "fire escape tag." The best fire escape was on the northeast corner of the building, by the classroom of Miss Van Cleve (who, you may remember, was the principal!). We would all have our rubber-soled Keds on and someone would be designated "It." Then we would start swinging like monkeys on the braces and beams of the fire escapes and tag each other until dark, when we couldn't see anymore. I don't recall anyone's being seriously injured, but I know if I had been a parent or grandparent of the players, I would have been petrified!

One or two nights a week, the American Legion Drum and Bugle Corps would practice and rehearse their routines under the lights of the football field, surrounded by the bleachers. We would all watch and imitate them.

Then when the lights were turned off, Horace Mann itself went to sleep, only to be awakened at 9 AM by a group of sleep-rested kids ready to go all-out again for another day!

My Adventures Expand

*Training for the show
with my prize beagle, Ace*

14.   Our Comical Neighbor, Perry

My father built our house some ten or twelve years before I was born there in 1925. It was a good house with a nice front yard and a porch with a swing. We had a living room, dining room, kitchen and a back porch on the first floor.

On the second floor, there were three bedrooms and a full bathroom. We had a full basement where Mom could hang her wash in bad weather, and there was a coal bin by the furnace.

The back porch housed our ice box, which my dad built. We also had a dining booth out there where we ate in the summertime.

Our dining room had a swinging door to the kitchen and a window that looked out into the back yard. There were also three windows above a buffet and they looked across the neighbor's driveway, into the three windows above *their* kitchen sink.

It was at those windows that our neighbor, a Mr. Perry Anderson, used to tap to get our attention at suppertime. He would entertain my sister and me with outlandish grimaces and funny faces.

As this story unfolds you will meet one of the most unforgettable characters -- and I do mean "characters!" -- of my life.

Perry and Blanche Anderson were our neighbors and I, as a child, never called them anything other than Mr. or Mrs. Anderson when I addressed them. But, in the privacy of our house, it was Perry and Blanche and for brevity's sake, I will refer to them as Perry and Blanche in my story.

They were both born in Bluffton, Ohio, about 15 miles from Lima. Bluffton was known for its Mennonite College, which is still going strong today. After college, Perry attended the College of Law at Ohio Northern University.

Blanche and Perry married late in life and never had any children. They were the only neighbors I knew to occupy their house in the 17 years that I lived next door.

Blanche was a staunch Pentecostal church member, but I never remember seeing Perry go to church. He was nonetheless a mild-mannered man and never swore. The only expletive I ever heard him utter if he were aggravated was "Piffle!" I don't think that he drank alcohol.

His only vice was that he smoked cigars and Blanche wouldn't let him smoke in the house, so he smoked on his front porch or out in the back yard.

Perry had his idiosyncrasies, one of which was to shout "Oh Yeah!" (pronounced "oh-YAY-uh!") at times when asked a question.

Neither Perry nor Blanche drove an automobile. Blanche had a sister who married a banker in town, and she used to come and visit Blanche in a little electric Phaeton. Perry's law office was downtown and he had to walk a couple of blocks to catch the street car to go to work. When the electric street cars were phased out, Perry really had it made, because the city bus then began to stop right across the street from his house.

Perry did mostly deeds and wills and absolutely refused to handle a divorce case! He would have his secretary show clients the door if they even mentioned divorce.

Perry's one passion was fishing. Since he had no automobile, he was dependent upon his fishing buddies for transportation. His closest angler friends were a man named Harry Wright and his wife, who lived on a farm not far from town.

Every couple of years, Perry and friends would take a trip to their favorite place, Lake Mindemoya on the Manitoulin Island in Lake Huron. Now, back in the 30's, this was a major undertaking. Many were the hours I spent on his front porch, listening to him tell how they would drive up to Mackinac and take a ferry across the Straits of Mackinac to the Upper Peninsula of Michigan.

Then they'd drive on to Sault Sainte-Marie. There they would cross over into Canada and head East on Highway 17 to Thessalon. From there, they took a train to Little Current on the Manitoulin Island, where they would be met by horses and wagons for the final trip to Lake Mindemoya and their cottages at the Maple Grove Resort.

Since Perry didn't furnish a car or do any of the driving, it became his responsibility to provide the

73

night crawlers or, as the Canadians called them, the "dew worms."

That is where I came into the picture. I was the Andersons' boy-in-residence. I mowed their lawn with a reel-type push mower for 50 cents a week. Perry liked the grass kept short so that when he and I would stalk the lightening-fast night crawlers, it would be easier to grab them.

He would water the grass in *his* front yard, and I would water the grass in *our* front yard. Then about nine o'clock at night we would both go on our hands and knees, with a flashlight in one hand, grabbing the elusive night crawlers with the other hand.

(I had trouble titling this piece. I didn't know whether to call it "Hunting Night Crawlers for Fun and Profit " or "What Do Dew Worms Do at Night?")

On Sunday afternoons, Perry would whistle for me and my good old beagle, Queen. Armed with buckets and trowels, we would walk the couple of blocks west to Baxter's Woods. There we would search the north sides of all the oak, beech, hickory and walnut trees for the soft green moss growing there. We would harvest all the moss we could, place it into the buckets, and head for home.

At home, Perry would take over. He would sort and grade the moss and add water to it to ensure moisture so that the worms to be added to it would find it a hospitable habitat. Since Perry had no car, his garage was the perfect work place for him to sort the worms -- small, medium, and large -- and to discard the sickly-appearing ones. He would hold weekly inspections as we would gather more dew worms and prepare them for the long trip north.

Perry was always searching for easier ways to harvest night crawlers, and here I must digress a bit so that this saga can continue:

My mother loved black walnuts, but the hulls on them were often quite adherent and tough to get off. So she devised a unique way of cracking the outer hull and removing the walnut. She would get a large burlap bag, fill it about half-full with the nuts in their hulls, flatten them out in the sack, then run her car over the sack, back and forth. The car wheels just peeled the hulls right off the nuts!

Then, she would put on heavy rubber gloves and pick the walnuts and throw then into a washtub. She would fill the tub with water to rinse off the staining walnut juice, so as not to get the stain on her hands. Then she could dispose of the burlap bag with the hulls and finish up by pouring out the rinse water onto the grass in the back yard. Shortly thereafter, the grass would be alive with night crawlers, even in the daytime! The juice apparently irritated them, and out they came.

Of course this happened in the fall, and was of no benefit to Perry, because he would only fish in the summertime and wouldn't fish even around Lima in the fall. But we did tell and show him the results. He filled several Mason jars with the juice from some of his own subsequent washings, and saved them in his basement.

The next summer, Perry got out his walnut juice and poured a couple jars of it onto the middle of his front yard. Nothing happened. The next day when he awakened, there was a huge brown area of dead grass in the middle the yard! He hadn't diluted the walnut juice as much as we had, and it killed his grass. He couldn't get grass to grow there for a couple of years!

The next thing Perry did to try to get the night crawlers to come out was also a miserable failure. Someone had given him a sure-fire worm extractor. It was a long electric cord with a male plug on one end to insert into an electric socket. At the other end, the cord split into two separate wires, each with a wooden insulating handle and a long stiff wire probe. The idea was to wet the grass and yard, then insert the probes into the turf about two or three feet apart, and then plug in the electric outlet.

Perry had given the electric plug to Blanche and told her not to plug it in till she heard him holler. I came up just as Perry had picked up the probes and was preparing to stick them into the turf. I asked Perry if he was trying something new and he gave out one of his "Oh YAY-uh"'s.

Blanche thought that was her signal, so she plugged the cord into the socket. About that time, Perry inadvertently touched the two probes together and there was a blinding flash, and all the lights in the Anderson house went off!

- - -

Well, the payoff for me was always when Perry would get home from his fishing trip. In the evenings after supper, Perry would hold court on his front porch where I sat on his swing. Between puffs on his cigar, he would hold me in fascination with tale after tale of the walleyes, jumbo perch, whitefish, and northern pike that had been caught. He'd tell of the storms that drove them in off the water, and of the mosquitoes.

I always hoped that I would get invited on one of those trips, but it never happened.

But at least I learned what dew worms do at night and I made 50 cents a week mowing Perry's grass.

15. My Newspaperin' Days

Frequently, kids are surprised to learn that our generation grew up before television, touch tone phones, computers, and global positioning satellites. There was indeed *LIFE* (and a whole magazine titled just after that fact) before all those inventions.

There were newscasters before Tom Brokaw, Dan Rather and Peter Jennings. *We* had Lowell Thomas and Walter Winchell.

There was comedy before "M*A*S*H," "Seinfeld," Archie Bunker and "Frasier." *We* had "Amos N' Andy," "Lum and Abner," and "One Man's Family."

There were sports before ESPN. People like Ronald Reagan used to read play-by-play baseball games from a ticker tape, and Red Barber used to broadcast football games live, such as the Notre Dame versus Southern California game.

Before there was CNN, C-Span, the Weather Channel, national availability of the *New York Times*, the *Washington Post* and *USA Today*, we had the *Toledo Blade*, the *Columbus Dispatch* and the *Lima News*.

In Lima, we didn't have Barbara Walters, Jane Pauley, or Paula Zahn, but *we* had . . . Ruth Creviston!

? ? ?

Well, Ruth, you may remember, was the mom of one of my best friends, Bob. Earl and Ruth Creviston, with son, Bob, and daughter, Lavina Ruth, lived two doors east of us. Earl, and several brothers, inherited a lumber yard and a hardware store, which supported their families, but over time the business gradually folded and was lost from the scene.

Ruth had had polio early in life and walked, as we have said previously, with a pronounced limp. She had graduated from Ohio Wesleyan University and had a degree in education and a teaching certificate. In those days, married women could not be hired as full-time teachers, but the schools were more than glad to have them as substitutes. And so it was in this capacity that Ruth did school teaching.

Due to her infirmity, Ruth could not drive a car, and was pretty much house-confined. But she always had her radio on and was the first in the neighborhood to hear any breaking news.

Like our family, Crevistons had enough to get by, but any extra money was always welcome. So whenever any big news story broke over the radio, Ruth would call the *Lima News* to see if they were going to put out an "EXTRA EDITION" and, if so, when would the papers be available? When she got a favorable answer, she would go out on her front porch and call loudly and frantically for Bob.

Since Bob and I were frequently together, we would both show up and come running to the porch and she would tell us of the breaking news story, and tell us to get some change to buy papers with and get on our bikes and get down to the *Lima News* so we could be first in line.

We would buy about 15 or 20 papers (for five cents each, then), head for the residential neighborhoods and start shouting things like *"Extra! Extra! The Hindenburg Dirigible Explodes in New Jersey – Read all about it! -- Read all about it!"*

We sold papers about the Lindbergh kidnapping case (1932-1935), Will Rogers and Wiley Post's crashing in Alaska (1935), the Hindenburg (1937), and many other happenings. People would come out and ask, "How much?" and we would say, "25 cents!" and if they would start to walk away, we'd come down to a dime.

Those were exciting, heady times, selling extras, and it became every boy's desire to acquire a *Lima News* route. However, they were hard to come by and were often passed down from brother to brother in a family. I remember that our paper boy, a Virgil Mousa, kept his route until he graduated from high school.

One day I heard that the *Columbus Dispatch* was looking for a carrier, so I went to what seemed a rather seedy area of town, down by the Lima Rescue Mission, to inquire about it. The man in charge said that he didn't have a route right then but that one might open up soon. Meanwhile, he suggested that I just sell papers out on the downtown streets on Fridays and Saturdays when farmers and rural people came to town. So I would take an armload of papers and head for High and Main Streets and the Public Square.

At first, it seemed that no one was interested in a *Columbus Dispatch*, so I thought I'd use the skills I had learned in selling Extras. I'd look through the paper and find an obscure article and amplify it: "*Woman shoots husband on neighbor's back porch! Read all about it!*"

Usually the item wasn't on the front page and if customers complained that it wasn't there, I told them to just look for it inside, and that it would be there.

80

With my "hype" approach, I sold more papers on the streets than some of the guys did with routes!

Eventually I was rewarded (if the word fits) with a route of 27 customers on the east side of town. But I lived three miles west of the customers.

Many of the customers only took the paper because they had an insurance policy with the *Columbus Dispatch* and were required to take it. Collecting for my papers from these customers was quite an education and I heard every reason on earth why they didn't have the 75 cents for the paper.

My bicycle was an old "single-tired" bike with skinny, narrow tires (vs. the bikes with double-thick balloon tires that supposedly gave a softer ride) and with no fenders that my dad used to ride to work during WWI. Frequently, the chain would break and I would be in a pickle.

Luckily, Dad was the foreman on the construction of the new Stadium, a WPA project, in east Lima. When the chain broke, I would push my bike to the construction site, find Dad, tell him my troubles, then he would put my bike in the trunk of his car and, when he got off work, he would take me around the rest of my route.

Lima Stadium, my emergency bike stop

On Sundays, I had to deliver the paper early in the morning. Mom didn't like me out there at that hour and, often, in the fall and winter, she would take me around the route in her car. She and Dad were both glad when I gave up that paper route, but I did save enough from it to buy myself a new bike with fenders.

On Saturdays, I would have to go to the little office and pay my bill for the papers I had delivered. If the collections were good on Friday, I would have a little money left over. There was a small novelty store not too far from the paper office, and I would go in there and treat myself to an ice cream cone. It wasn't till some time later that someone intimated to me that the "novelty store'" might actually be a front for a house of prostitution, run by a very attractive, well-known woman of some renown in Lima.

I got some good experience from both the street selling and the route selling of papers. I met some nice people and some grouches, and, here again, as in my friendship with Eldon, I got an education in human relations that is not written in textbooks.

I guess I really have to thank Ruth Creviston for the beginning of my newspaperin' experience. But Ruth did much more for me. My folks hadn't gone past the eighth grade in school and so it was Ruth who guided and advised me into the college prep course. She insisted that I take Latin, German, chemistry and physics in school.

When I returned to Lima years later to practice medicine, it was my privilege to care for Ruth and her handicapped daughter until they heeded my advice and moved to Florida into a lifetime care community in Bradenton.

There is an epilogue to this story: the newspapers weren't done with me yet. One year, some friends, who thought that I could be of help talked me into running for the school board in Lima. Both newspapers ran editorials stating that a brash, young physician might upset the status quo too much.

They endorsed the incumbent board members.

But apparently their newspaper opinions didn't amount to much because I won by a landslide. One of the detracting editors even became my patient later and I cared for him until he died in his 80s of a chronic illness.

So how's *that* for *"EXTRA! EXTRA! Get your hot news here!"*?

16.   A Tribute to Uncle Charlie

Most of us have had a favorite uncle or aunt as we were growing up.   My favorite uncle was Charles Shilling, who was married to Lula Showalter, my mother's older sister.

Uncle Charlie and Aunt Lu lived about 25 miles northeast of Lima.

Lula and Charlie,
wedding picture, 1911

They lived on an 80-acre farm, where they grew corn, wheat, oats, soy- beans, and alfalfa hay.   Charlie also had five or six milk cows, and hogs, both for market and for their own use. Aunt Lu raised white leghorn chickens for eggs and for frying chicken, and she had a big garden.   In addition to all this, Uncle Charlie drove a rural school bus.

They had a large windmill and tower adjacent to their house that supported a most wondrous grape arbor that grew the most delicious white grapes that were so refreshing when you came in out of a hot field!

Uncle Charlie and Aunt Lu had two children, a boy named Russell, and a girl named Roberta.   I never met or knew Russell, as he died of meningitis.   He had been the light of Uncle Charlie's life, and his loss was a

84

terrible blow. Perhaps that is why Uncle Charlie was always so friendly to me, as I must have represented the boy he lost, and longed for.

Russell   Roberta

Uncle Charlie would frequently ask me when I was going to come up and help him on the farm. I always thought he was kidding me, but, as I got older and bigger and could really be of some use to him, I realized that he would really like for me to come. My mom and dad urged me to go and stay for a week and see what life on the farm was like. They promised to come and get me right on schedule, so I decided to try it early one summer, when Uncle Charlie was ready to make hay.

For those without much farming background, perhaps I should explain the difference between straw and hay, since people sometimes confuse the two. Straw is for bedding; hay is for food.

Straw is the dried stalks of wheat or oats after it is harvested. The threshing machine was used to blow the straw into huge stacks called straw stacks. The straw would be used throughout the year as bedding

85

for the cows, horses, sheep, and also in the chicken houses for nests. Straw is not food for the cattle and horses. They won't eat it, so it makes excellent bedding in the stables and milking barn. Sometimes they appear to want to eat it when it is baled because a stalk of wheat, say, that is loaded with grain will get into the bale by mistake and stick out and attract the cows' interest. But there's no nutrition in straw and animals basically don't eat it.

Hay is usually made from alfalfa (or red or sweet clover, or timothy, or mixtures of the three), and when Uncle Charlie would have to get the field crop ready to be turned into hay, he'd mow it down, and then rake it into windrows with a side-delivery rake. Then he always had to let the hay cure in the field for a day or so, depending on the weather and drying conditions.

At waiting times like that, when there was nothing for me to do in the field, Aunt Lu would get me aside and we would take off in the old Chevy and sneak over to New Stark. New Stark was just a little wide spot in U.S. 30, where there was a small general store that sold ice. Aunt Lu would get vanilla or lemon extract and put a 25-pound chunk of ice on the bumper of the car.

Then we would head back to the farm, where we would chip the ice into pieces. Aunt Lu would fill a metal freezing container with the vanilla or lemon mixture she'd made and we would pack ice and rock salt around it. Then I would hand-crank the freezer till I couldn't turn it any more. And that night after supper, we would surprise Uncle Charlie with a big bowl of homemade ice cream, his favorite dessert. We would all eat ice cream all evening because they didn't have a refrigerator with a freezing compartment for keeping it solid and we had to eat it all before bedtime. I never met a man who liked ice cream better than Uncle Charlie.

The next day, we would usually be ready to start on the hay once it had dried. Uncle Charlie would hook the hay loader onto the back of the hay wagon, and then he would teach me how to drive old Maude and Jack, his beloved team of mules. I would drive the wagon down the windrows of hay while he took the hay coming up from the hay loader and placed it on the wagon to make an even load.

Once we had a wagonload, we would unhook the hay loader from it and head for the barn. Uncle Charlie would back the wagon into the barn. Then he unhitched the mules from the wagon and re-hitched them to the ropes and pulleys hanging in the barn.

He taught me how to stick the hayforks into the hay to hold it together, and then he would drive the mules forward and pull the hay up into the haymow. I would pull the trip rope and dump the load where we wanted it in the mow. Then we would start all over.

That was really an enjoyable thing for this city boy to learn. I felt so proud to be useful. I loved it!

Towards the end of the week, I was getting a little homesick and would go out in the front yard looking down the road for my folks' car.

Over the span of five or six years, Uncle Charlie introduced me to so many things! I learned about the "threshing circles" which were groups of 10 or 12 farmers who would join together to help harvest each other's crops of wheat and oats, with tremendous dinners at noon that the farm wives prepared for the men. I learned about de-tasseling hybrid corn for seed producers. I learned about butchering hogs in the winter. But one of the best things I learned from Uncle Charlie was hunting and sportsmanship.

Uncle Charlie was a staunch conservationist. Woe be unto any hunter who shot a hen pheasant or exceeded the daily bag limit of pheasants or rabbits. They would never again be allowed to hunt on Uncle Charlie's land. When the winters were severe, he would carry buckets of shelled corn back to the woods for the pheasants, squirrels, and rabbits. He would make brush piles, and would always let his fence rows grow to give nesting cover for the birds.

In the latter part of 1942, when I was 17, Uncle Charlie became ill, and on Jan 20, 1943, a month after his daughter, Roberta, was married, he passed away.

I remember telling my dad the news as he got home from work that day. It was the first time I had ever seen him weep, as he and Charlie were the closest of friends. The funeral was in the same church where Roberta had just been married.

In those days, the body always lay in state in the living room of the family home. On the day of the funeral, I was standing out in the middle of the road as the pallbearers brought the casket from the house to the funeral coach.

Just as they were placing the casket into the hearse, a rooster and a hen pheasant came up out of the ditch and cackled as they flew directly over the casket as it was being loaded.

At that moment, I knew that Uncle Charlie was in God's hands, and that He had sent two messengers to assure us all, and to pay a last and fitting tribute to Uncle Charlie.

Aunt Lula and Uncle Charlie, after 30 years of marriage, 1941

I waited almost 60 years to write this, and it has been in my memory bank ever since the funeral and the pheasant flyover. This story puts me in memory of more tales about my interactions with Uncle Charlie and Aunt Lu, and I will be sharing those later in this book.

17. Some of My Best Friends Were Dogs

Many a happy day during my growing-up years was spent playing with our pet dogs. Let me tell you about them.

The first dog that came into my life was named Queen. She was an older beagle, with popping eyes and a gray muzzle. She was a three-family dog, with Speidels to the west, and the Murrays and Perry Anderson to the east. She would lie in whichever back yard had the most shade. Unfortunately, she got prime table scraps from both sides and became too fat to run rabbits well.

Perry Anderson would come out his back door and give a melodious whistle reserved for Queen. If she was in our house, she would be frantic until we let her out. Then off she would go with Perry to Baxter's woods. Perry would harvest green moss for his Dew worms while Queen sniffed for rabbits. They would return in a couple of hours, and both had their tongues hanging out.

Queen died one morning while I was in school and when I came home at noon, I was devastated to have lost my dear old friend. But Perry was equally as devastated and missed her as much as I did.

My dad also missed having a beagle around the house. He liked to take them out to listen to them "bell" as they would chase a rabbit. I think I was about 10 years old at around this time because it was in 1935 that MacKinlay Kantor's book, *The Voice of Bugle Ann*, came out. I got it from the library and read it, and had Dad read it, too. This book was about a foxhound named Bugle Ann with a beautiful "belling" voice. And a foxhound actually looks like an oversized beagle and stands about 20 inches at the shoulder, while the largest Beagles are 15 inches or less in stature.

Well, that book stoked my Dad's fire. And so, one Sunday found Dad, Mom and me on our way to Cincinnati to a sporting dog show. The highways were very icy and when we got to Piqua, about 40 miles from home, Mom wanted to turn around and go home. However, Dad persisted and we drove the 120 miles to the dog show.

There we saw a perky little beagle who was such a friendly little dog, and he won his class in the show, though not Best Of Breed for the beagles. Dad went over and talked to the owner, who had several dogs in the show.

The dog we liked was AKC-registered (American Kennel Club) under the name of "War Cry the Second." He had won several field trials and several bench shows, but his owner thought that he was a little temperamental and wasn't good enough to become a Field Trial Champion, which is what he wanted. Dad got the owner's name, address, and phone number and the asking price for this little gem of a dog.

All the way back to Lima, all Dad and I could talk about was this wonderful little dog. Mom said he was nice, but she didn't know if we could afford $35 for a dog. In 1935, that was a *chunk*. But Dad pestered Mom long enough till she gave in. He wrote the owner, sent him a check and the owner sent us our "dream dog" by Railway Express.

91

What a joy it was when I came home from school one day and there he was, AKC papers and all. "War Cry the Second" he was indeed, but as his owner explained to us, he would only answer to the name of "Ace."

Things went well until one winter's day when my mom came home from the store. She came in our side door, set her bags of groceries down on the floor, went to the front door and got the evening newspaper. She took off her coat and stood over a hot air register to get warm while she read the obituary columns.

Suddenly, she became aware of the sound of paper rustling and she went to check her bags of groceries. There she witnessed Ace just finishing off a pound of bacon. She let out a whoop, rolled up the newspaper and chased the poor dog from the kitchen to the dining room, to the living room and then back out to the kitchen, swatting him with the newspaper. The poor dog got so upset that he vomited the bacon on the living room carpet.

Then I had to rescue him and take him out to his kennel. Mom wouldn't let him back in the house for a week, but they finally made up.

Dad had been talking about having a brace, or pair, of beagles to hunt together, and so he also bought a dog a little taller than Ace. His name was Vick.

When a beagle is hunting, his tail is referred to as his "flag" and sometimes when he is hunting in heavy brush, all you can see is his flag. Vick had a good flag, but he wasn't near the hunter that Ace was, and he was a little mean to Ace. So Dad traded Vick for another dog named Sniffer.

This dog looked more like a basset hound than a beagle and, because of his shorter legs, he was much slower.

I had really been impressed by that dog show in Cincy where we found our Ace. One day I saw an article in our paper that there was going be a Sporting Dog Show on Labor Day over in Dunkirk, at the Leafy Oaks Coon Dog Field Trials. Colonel Leon Robinson was sponsoring the show, it said. I thought I would write and get the details.

I prevailed upon Mom and Dad to let me enter Ace in the show. I sent in the registration and the entry fees. I had about a month to work with Ace, trotting him on leash, and teaching him to stand still on the bench, hold up his tail, and not to flinch when the judge would lift his lips to check his teeth.

While I was working with Ace, my oldest brother would smirk and gave me reason after reason why I was wasting my time. He said Ace's muzzle wasn't trim enough, so I took Dad's barber scissors and cut Ace's whiskers flush.

Well. the day came. Mom, Dad and I went to Dunkirk along with Ace to the Dog show. I won't drag it out, but suffice it to say that Ace won Best of Class, Best of Breed, and went on to win *Best of Show*!

When we got home, my formerly-scornful brother opined that he had given me the right pointers to produce a show winner.

This was heady stuff for an 11 year old kid!

"Best of Show" – we did it!

The next spring I read about another big Sporting Dog Show to be held in Ravenna, Ohio, in the early summer. It was to be held in the middle of the week, and Dad had to work, but I successfully prevailed upon Mom to take me and Ace to the show.

It was about 100 miles away and we got there in time, but I found out that most of the men and women showing dogs were professionals and made their living doing this. Well, Ace and I became the "sentimental favorites" of the crowd, and when Ace won Best of Class and Best of Breed, I had a regular cheering section when it came time for the Best of Show competition.

I had to go to the restroom so I had Mom hold Ace's leash. When I was in there, I overheard the judge talking to some men and one said "We can't let this kid walk away with this prize, or the trainers won't be back next year." They called for the finalist dogs in the Best of Show category to enter the arena and Ace strutted like he knew what to do to win, and the crowd was with us.

However, a beautiful Irish setter was awarded Best of Show and Ace got second place. The judge called us aside and congratulated us and suggested that I get cinders into his run to toughen his feet and make him more bouncy, and other things. I just smiled up at him and said, "I understand."

We didn't get home till about 11 o'clock, and my dad and brothers were worried sick. They had called the Highway Patrol and Sheriff's Department to see if there had been any accidents reported. That was the last show for Ace and me.

Another beagle owner in our area had seen Ace, and propositioned Dad to have Ace sire some puppies from his female. The terms were that we would get the pick of the litter. Came the day, and Dad and I went to pick up the puppy, and there was a male pup, the spitting image of Ace. And so we took possession of War Cry III

He was later to be called "Pippy," for 2 reasons:

1} He was a Pip of a pup, and

2} He "pippyed" on the floor rather than on the newspapers.

When Pippy came, we sold Sniffer, and so we just had two dogs, father and son. Since we had to concern ourselves with Pippy's education, Dad helped me make a lightweight trailer mounted on bicycle wheels that I could pull easily behind my bike.

I would load the two dogs into their trailer, fasten it to my bike, and off we would go, out to Robb Avenue, and then on farther west about a quarter of a mile. There we would find a lane that had been worn into the ground by ruts, and we would go on back into the woods and brambles. (I think this area, years later, was developed, and became Edgewood Estates). Ace was the teacher and Pippy was the pupil, and together they made beautiful music trailing rabbits.

The next November, when hunting season was just a week off, I began making plans to get out of school on opening day so I could go hunting with my dad and brothers. I had acquired a new Ithaca Featherlite 20-gauge pump shotgun, and I was most anxious to try it out.

The school principal said I could not get out until noon of opening day. But Dad and my brothers said they couldn't wait until then because they were going about fifty miles northeast where the pheasants were most plentiful. Since they wouldn't wait for me, when I got home at noon, I put the dogs in their trailer, slung my shotgun in its case over my shoulder, and we went off to our usual Robb Avenue training grounds.

That afternoon, I got two cock pheasants and two rabbits and I put my dogs in their trailer and we went triumphantly home. About three hours later, my Dad and brothers returned, and they had been "skunked." I didn't let them forget my prowess for quite a while.

When my folks moved out to their new house and farm on Stewart Road, Pippy wasn't used to the speeding vehicles on the country road and he got hit by a car. We took him to one of my childhood heroes, Dr. Joseph Morris, our veterinarian. It turned out that Pippy was lucky and only had a lower spine injury. However, this resulted in a paralyzed tail and from then on, when he hunted, we could never see his flag.

- - -

I had gone to college in l943 and one day I got a letter from Mom telling me that Ace had died, and Dad had buried him underneath a beautiful big elm tree in our pasture about 100 yards from the barn.

The next time I went home, I went up to the barn to help out, and saw Pippy sitting beside Ace's grave. We called him and he trotted very slowly to us, while looking back at the grave.

- - -

Back at college I was called to active Army duty and a flurry of travel. I had basic training in Texas and X-ray technology school in Atlanta. Then, after a 10-day furlough home to visit Mom, Dad, and Pippy, I returned to Camp Barkley, Texas, and was assigned to the 241st General Hospital. They moved me by train to Camp Kilmer, New Jersey, a staging area for preparing to go overseas. We then embarked on the *Ile de France*, the largest existing passenger ship at that time, which had been commandeered as a troop transport. It took us nine days to cross the Atlantic and we docked in Greenoch, Scotland. From there, we went to Knutsford, England for a month, awaiting orders to cross the English Channel. Then we sailed for France on New Years Eve, 1944, and landed in Cherborg, France in the middle of a driving snowstorm.

- - -

While I was in France, I got word from Mom that Pippy had died and that Dad had buried him beside Ace, his father.

And so, sadly, my friends, the Dog Days of My Youth came to a close.

18. My Jobs as a Boy in the 1930's

When I was a kid, my two brothers were eight and ten years older than me. My oldest brother, Marvin, went off to college in 1935, when I was only ten.

My other brother, Ken, opted not to finish his senior year of high school and got a job. Unfortunately, in 1941 when the military draft was started, he was among the first numbers drawn, and he went off to military service.

I also had a sister, Mary, but she had to be gone for nine months out of the year, as she attended the Ohio State School for the Deaf.

Accordingly, I grew up almost as an only child. I had quite a few duties, chores and obligations that were expected of me around the house, but that will be material for a future story.

I never got a set allowance, so if I wanted any spending money of my own, I had to earn it by doing odd jobs. I don't want to imply that I had a Spartan existence. My parents supplied all that I needed and were generous in their care of me.

Mom gave me 25 cents for mowing the grass each time, and for shoveling snow, whenever that needed doing.   And so snow shoveling and grass mowing for our neighbors was probably my earliest source of outside pocket money.   Occasionally, a housewife in the neigh-borhood would hire me to clean her basement or garage or to rake leaves.

My problem was that I didn't know how much to ask for my labors. In one case, a lady gave me a wood-shafted mid-iron golf club for cleaning her basement. I thus got a chance to knock some golf balls around the nearby college grounds.

One year, I got a job with a small grocery store called Harris's Grocery. They hired me to deliver handbills on Friday after school, announcing their specials for Saturday. They must have done all right because, within a year, they closed that little store and moved about a mile away, where they became Harris's IGA Market. I wasn't disappointed to lose the work, as that hand bill job had entailed a *LOT* of walking, and unfriendly dogs, too.

Twice a year, Spring and Fall, I would get two or three days' work with the Lima Telephone and Telegraph Company, delivering new phone books. I had a wagon, which was required for the job, and I would fill it with pre-addressed phonebooks, walk to the appropriate neighborhood, deliver the new books, then walk back to the phone company with the returned old books and get a new load. I don't recall what the pay scale was, but I remember they would give us a small brown envelope with our wages in cash. What a great feeling that was!

Shortly after I got my driving permit, I got a job with the Collett Street Market delivering groceries on Fridays and Saturdays using their panel truck. I also helped fill orders that were phoned in by the customers.

One day, I was filling an order and I got stumped. I couldn't make out an item, so I went to the owner's wife who had taken the order. She roared with laughter and said, "That is Fine Art Facial Soap." She had abbreviated it to read "F.Art" soap.

In the beginning of the summer, after my freshman year in high school, I looked at the want ads and saw that the J. F. Renz Bakery on North Main, across from the Courthouse, wanted a baker's helper. I went down and interviewed for the job and got it. I then had to buy some white pants and white shirts.

When I went to work, they ushered me up to the second floor and introduced me to the bakers, and I went to work. They patiently instructed me in the art of making glazed donuts and pies. We made all sizes of pie, but mostly made those little "nickel" or five-cent pies. I also served time on the bread ovens and wrapping machines.

When quitting time came, they all hung up their aprons and prepared to leave. As I began to leave, they told me, "No, no! The bakers' helper is required to wash up all the [huge] kettles, pots, and pans before he leaves." What a revoltin' development! I was there for another three hours getting things ready for the next day.

As the weather turned warmer, the heat in the bakery became sweltering. I could only endure that job for a couple of weeks while I was searching the want ads for a more comfortable job.

Then I spied just the job I wanted: the Lima Ice and Coal Company wanted two high school boys to work on the dock and sell ice, and to help with the frozen food lockers. After the broiling heat of the bakery, I was definitely looking for a cooler job, so I went to their office. I was interviewed by Harley Kesler, the owner, and was hired. Then I went back to the bakery and terminated my services.

100

The job at the Lima Ice and Coal Company was from 4 PM till midnight, six days a week. It paid 25 cents an hour, and involved a number of different jobs: first, the selling of both block and crushed ice to customers; second, checking the ice truck drivers in and out with their ice; and, third, using a hoist to pull the large tanks of frozen water up out of the freezing-brine vat, and then extracting the 300-pound chunks of ice from the container.

Once one of these huge ice chunks had been pulled out, I had to run it through a "scoring saw machine," which outlined it with grooves for 25, 50, and 100-pound pieces. I would then slide it through a small door into the storage freezer. The last step was to go around into the storage freezer and stand the scored 300-pound piece up on end.

I wore heavy leather shoes to work, and the other guy they hired showed up with black Keds gym shoes. When people came in to buy ice, we most often put it up on their back bumper. You would put a corner of the chunk of ice in the hollow of the bumper and, if the driver didn't hit too many bumps, it would ride quite nicely. About the second week, my colleague hoisted a 50-pound block with his tongs up and onto a bumper, but both the bumper and the ice fell on his toes! Well, he was off for about two weeks and, when he came back, he was wearing steel-toed work shoes.

A lot of very brawny guys worked on the ice trucks. I once saw Harold Jennings, a friend of mine who went to South, our rival high school, take a 300-pound block of ice off the loading dock onto his shoulder, carry it up a flight of stairs, and set it down on the loading dock. Lesson learned? Don't mess with Harold Jennings!

101

The one thing I hated about the ice dock job was my bicycle ride home after midnight. From Elizabeth, I rode west on Wayne Street to Washington Street, and then down a three-quarter mile stretch of Delphos Road, which was along the railroad track, and unlit. My bike had no lights, either. The thing I dreaded most was passing by the Chiles and Son Funeral Home at midnight, then going down that long stretch of darkness.

Chiles had a little white low-slung ambulance, a CORD, made in Auburn, Indiana. It looked like it was doing 80 miles an hour when it was standing still and I always remembered it. I would always stand up and pump my bike for all I was worth until I cleared the funeral home. I didn't want to ride in that little white ambulance!

In my senior year in high school, my chemistry teacher, E. L. Huber, was approached by a Mr. O. B, Schultz, head of the testing lab at the Lima Locomotive works. He wanted a recommendation from Mr. Huber of a student who knew something of chemistry and handling glassware in a laboratory. Mr. Huber gave him my name and I went out to be interviewed by Mr. Schultz. He was a pleasant man in his fifties, an interesting individual who, among other things, played the oboe.

He outlined my duties, as follows: I was to work after school and on Saturdays. I was expected to:
1) nightly, to clean up the array of machines, drill presses, lathes and also the Brinnel machines which were used to test the tensile strength of steel; 2) when requested, to assist Giles Howell, the metallurgist; 3) to serve as an apprentice to Don Jardine, the photographer, and to keep the darkroom clean, to mix

102

his developer and hypo solutions, to ferrotype prints so as to produce a glossy finish, and to learn to make enlargements and prints.

There was a padlocked gate near the testing lab on 4th Street, I was told; I could park my car there and come in that gate. It was then that I decided to buy my first car, a 1935 Dodge coupe, for $200, from my dad.

I helped make X-rays of castings using a plumb bob filled with radium. The procedure was carried out by the metallurgist, and a single radiograph might take 24 to 48 hours to expose. I then would develop the film, removing it from its cardboard holder for processing.

The lab was a low-key place to work, considering the plant was making Sherman Tanks for the Army. I worked there till I graduated from high school, then I had to leave to enroll in college at Ohio State University. As it turned out, Don Jardine, the man for whom I had worked at the Lima Loco, moved to California shortly after I left the job. As I understand it, one of his, then, small sons, Al(an) Jardine, went on to become one of the original "Beach Boys."

And, as for me, who would have guessed that, 12 years later, I would again be returning to the Lima Locomotive Works, but this time as the company doctor!

When I was at school in Columbus, I got a part-time job in the mail room at the Ohio Tuberculosis Association, sending out various promotional brochures and publications that had been ordered. This was in the basement of a big house on Neil Avenue.

And when I went home at Christmas break, I got a job at the Lima Post Office delivering packages with another student. We worked out of the back of a State Highway Truck. The job only lasted 2 weeks . . . another cold job.

Then I went back to college, expecting to continue much as before. But soon I began my longest job ever! In February of 1944, on Valentine's Day, I was called to duty by the U.S. Army Enlisted Reserve Corps. It offered a two-and-a-half year tour of Europe, all expenses paid, and $50 a month.

What a deal!

19. My First Cigarette at the Football Game

The street my house was on was the northern dead-end point for College Avenue. That two-block area between College and Jameson Avenues was where Horace Mann School was, and also the Central High School Athletic addition. To the south of those buildings were the football field and bleachers, called the "College Field."

Just east of the football field were the only clay tennis courts in all of Lima (as described in Chapter 13, "The Playground at Horace Mann School").

When I was about six years old, I really welcomed the football season. It was one of the most exciting times of the year for me! I got to watch the practices and scrimmages of both the varsity and the freshman teams.

When Lima Central was having a home game, I would get up on Saturday morning, eat breakfast, and be over at the College Field by 8 AM. Eli A. Hauenstein, who was the building and grounds manager for the Central Dragons, would be at the main gate.

Every kid in the neighborhoods would gather around Mr. Hauenstein. He would shout out instructions and have the kids line up with their backs against the east fence, which separated the tennis courts from the refreshment stand. During the game and at half time you could get hot dogs, pop, coffee and hot chocolate at the concession area. I got something else there, as you shall see.

We spaced ourselves an arm's length apart. Then Eli would get out in front of us, blow a whistle, and we would walk slowly in line to the opposite end of the field as we would pick up trash and debris. Some of us had to walk under the bleacher seats to pick up trash, and that was the best area because sometimes you would find a dime or a quarter.

After we got to the far end of the field, we would deposit the trash, walk single-file past Mr. Hauenstein, and receive one free general admission ticket to the game that afternoon.

Eli always stood by the single west gate, and when you got your ticket, you would walk out that gate. Then it was locked for the rest of the day. But I would still stay and watch for awhile.

With all the kids out, Mr. Hauenstein's assistants would begin to line the playing field with a lime applicator, marking the end lines, goal lines, side lines and every five-yard line. By the end of that, most of the morning would be gone, so I would go home for dinner (called lunch nowadays).

I would eat as quickly as I could, and then get out on the front porch and look for the buses of the visiting team. None of the schools back then had their own team bus, so they all chartered Greyhound or National Trailways buses. It was as exciting to me then to see a "GREYHOUND BUS" from Dayton, Defiance, or Bowling Green parked on Hazel Avenue as it would be for today's kids to see a jet fighter up close.

Well now, the excitement would continue to build as cars and people arrived to fill up the bleachers. The girls would have pennants and pompoms as they advanced toward College Field. You

106

could hear the pep bands playing and the cheerleaders exhorting their fans to loud and progressive cheers.

At about 1:30 PM, we would see the coin toss, and the kickoff followed. I never had a seat picked out, so Bob Creviston and I would wander around and people-watch.

On one rather cold Saturday (I don't remember who the visiting team was), Bob and I were wandering around the refreshment stand. We didn't have any money to buy anything, but it just smelled good there. A couple of the girls selling hotdogs suddenly got busy with a lot of customers and they each threw away a half-smoked cigarette.

Bob and I snatched up those two half-smoked cigarettes and scooted around behind the North bleachers. We started puffing away as we walked along behind the bleachers. All of a sudden, I found myself flat on my back looking up into the angry face of my older brother, Kenneth.

He had been sitting on the top row of seats, when his friend nudged him and said, "Look down there at your little brother." Ken came down the back side of the bleachers and pounced on me like a peregrine falcon on a pigeon. As soon as I was flattened, Bob Creviston pitched his cigarette and took off running out the main gate, and was gone.

Ken tore that cigarette out of my grasp and stood me up, swatted my seat, and said "Get on home!" I pulled myself together, climbed the west fence, went home and when I got there acted as though nothing had happened. The next morning, I was getting dressed for Sunday School when Mom came into the room and said, with one eyebrow raised, "I hear that you have decided to take up smoking!"

107

Well, the flood gates of tears opened. I hugged her skirts and promised, "I'll never do it again!" I had already been chastised by my brother and didn't need a spanking on top of that!

I kept my promise for many years, and even in the Army I didn't smoke. We were given two cigarettes with each K ration, and we could buy a carton a week from the PX (post exchange). I generally used cigarettes for bartering with the civilians.

Here are two anecdotes that show how cigarettes figured into my days of military service:

On New Year's Eve, December 31, 1944, our hospital, the 241st General, crossed the English Channel and landed at Cherborg, France. It was snowing and cold. We were loaded into trucks and taken to a little coastal town called Etretat. We couldn't tell much that night, but the next morning, we realized that we were living in the few structures left standing in a bombed-out town. (As it turned out, this was the birthplace of Victor Hugo.)

A couple of us thought we would go up on a cliff to inspect a partially-destroyed German machine-gun fortification. An old Frenchman stopped us from going up the path. He couldn't speak English and we couldn't speak French. He kept saying *"cent"* [one hundred] and drawing a C on the palm of his hand.

Then he pointed down to the ground, and there was the detonator for a land-mine sticking up. He had been trying to tell us that there were 100 land mines in the ground on either side of the path. He had saved our lives!

108

In a small attempt to show our thanks, I gave him a couple packs of cigarettes and he nodded in appreciation.

The next day, they loaded us onto trucks and took us to a railroad siding. We were waiting for a train to some destination we didn't know. While we were waiting, I sauntered alone over to a little bakery (*patisserie*).

Since the Germans had been there for five years, I assumed that these people understood German, so I tried to talk to them in my German from school, but they played dumb and said that they didn't speak any. So, I picked up a baguette about two feet long and said, "*Combien?*" ["how much?" in French]. They said a number in French which I didn't know, so I held out two packs of cigarettes and they smiled and nodded "*oui*".

I stuck the baguette down inside my overcoat and rejoined my comrades and said nothing of the barter. Eventually the train came and we were loaded into the "40 by 8" boxcars (this was GI slang coming from the inscription on the outside of the cars, which read *40 Hommes et 8 Cheveaux* – "40 Men and 8 Horses"). The weather had gotten bitterly cold. They slammed the door shut on our boxcar and the train began to move. There were many stops and starts all night long

Through some leaks that let light in, I could see that it was getting to be morning outside. I noticed that the breaths of our "40 men" had condensed and frozen on the walls and ceiling of our Pullman coach and that we were now in an icehouse.

I thought I would try to stand up from my sitting position but, alas, my overcoat was frozen fast to the wall and I couldn't get up. I then thought that I would have a swallow of water but when I reached for my canteen, it had frozen solid during the night. What a miserable state to be in!

I looked around, and no one else seemed awake, so I reached down inside my overcoat and broke off a chunk of the baguette, which was body-temperature warm. Angel food cake couldn't have tasted any better!

Later on, the train stopped and the door was opened. We all got out to walk around, have a nature call, and get some powdered scrambled eggs and coffee. Then it was back on the train.

It took us two days and two nights to go just 180 miles. They were only feeding us twice a day, but my secret bread kept me comforted the whole trip. They had to be careful because, as we found out, the Battle of the Bulge was on and a troop train would have been a sitting duck for the *Luftwaffe*.

Finally, we got off the train at a little town called Sisson not far from Rheims and the SHAEF (Supreme Headquarters, Allied Expeditionary Force). The 82nd Airborne Division was up in the bulge, and gone. So they moved our hospital into the 82nd's quarters and we began to take the wounded from the Bulge, which was only 30 miles away.

So you see I *did* keep my promise to Mom. I didn't smoke those cigarettes. But they had still come in handy, and saved me from misery and hunger when I was in tough straits.

Life in the '30s

Uncle Charlie on his farm

20. The Sounds of Lima in the 1930's

As I prepared to write this story, I tried to think back to the first sounds that I could remember growing up. Since we lived only two blocks from the Pennsylvania mainline and switchyards, the first sounds that I became aware of were probably:

The Railroad Sounds.

And what were those?

The switch engine, with its ding-ding bell, as it scurried back and forth cutting cars out of a freight train or adding cars to the train, or helping a freight train make it up the grade.

The freight locomotive's big drive wheels that would grind, and you would hear a chugg---chugg --- chugg in ever-increasing speed until the wheels would slip. Then, sand would be added to the track and the engine would start all over again until it gained speed and would proceed on down the track.

You would hear the speeding Broadway Limited, blaring its horn as it sped through town. If you were standing at the crossing, you would hear the clickety-clack as the huge iron wheels passed over a "joint "in the tracks.

The little two-man cars that the maintenance workers would use to inspect the tracks, called "Gandy cars"; you could hear these, too. We used to call them "putt-putt cars" because of their little gasoline

113

engines. In earlier days before they carried engines for power they were just called "hand-cars." (The Gandy cars were made by the Gandy Company in Chicago, which lent its name to the term "Gandy dancer." "Gandy dancer" used to refer to an operator of the car but gradually came to mean anyone who worked on the section gang.)

The crossings had different sounds. On East Market Street at the B&O tracks, a gate would come down and the lights would blink in time with the ding-ding-ding of the warning bells. Other crossings did not have gates, but only the flashing lights and the ding-ding sound. The freight trains would sound their mournful whistles and horns several hundred yards before each of the crossings all the way through town. We also had a couple of underpasses and it was always eerie going through the underpass when a train was going over it up above.

Then there were the *Street Sounds*:

I can remember as a young boy, lying in bed, hearing the clop-clop-clop of the hoof beats of the horse pulling the milk wagon. The hoof beats would stop out front and then I would hear the rattling of bottles in the metal basket as the milkman came up the sidewalk. I'd hear his steps on the porch, the exchange of full bottles for empty bottles, then the tinkling retreat to the milk wagon and the resumption of clop-clop-clop to the next stop.

When I lived on Hazel Avenue, the street itself was red brick. The metal tires on the wheels of the milk wagons made a distinct metallic, grinding, clicking sound. And heavy trucks on the brick pavement produced a humming sound. College Avenue dead-ended onto Hazel and it was an asphalt street (wonderful for skating) and, at nights, I could hear a truck coming almost silently down that asphalt and then the distinctive "humm" as it turned onto the brick street.

Another street sound was the electric street cars with their warning clanging bell, and you could even hear and sense the swaying motion from the bell as the car went along. At the end of the line, on Jameson Avenue in front of Horace Mann school, the conductor would switch the train's direction. He would open the front window and reach out and hook the trolley up to the power wire. Then he would carry the fare box to the other end of the car, open that window, and take off the trolley connection on that end. Then he would walk the length of the car again, reversing the seats with a series of loud metallic thumps.

In the spring and summer, Vincent Rinella would drive his horse and wagon up and down the streets of the neighborhoods and shout " Ba-- - na---- nas!" to offer his produce to the housewives. There was another man who used to drive his horse and wagon through the neighborhoods, shouting "Old Raggs...Old Baggs...Old Iron!" and he would take your junk away for you.

The Barr Hotel Pastry truck was always a welcome sound with its characteristic CLANG-- CLANG--CLANG. Housewives and children would come running out of their houses to hail the driver down to buy glazed donuts, jelly rolls, éclairs, breads, pies and cakes. Not only did his truck have a distinctive sound, but he also had the most wonderful aroma when he opened his back doors to display the goodies.

Two or three times a year, a street sweeper would come up and down our brick street with a vigorous BRUSSHHING sound. The streets always looked dirtier when he was done than before he started!

On Fridays (was it every Friday, or just the first or last Friday of the month?), the Solar Refinery would sound its tremendously *LOUD SIREN* at noon. The kids always used to shout "Payday at the Refinery!", but I doubt if the employees needed a siren to tell them when it was payday. I think it was to synchronize all the clocks.

In the spring you could hear the Thunk...Thunk of a rug beater applied to the living and dining room carpets on the backyard clothes line. It never ceased to amaze me how much dust and dirt came out of those carpets, despite their having been vacuumed weekly by the trusty Hoover or Eureka cleaning machines during the winter.

In summer, one would hear the familiar sound of a reel-type hand mower, and smell the aroma of fresh-cut grass.

Also, in the summer you could hear the familiar noise of coal being shoveled into someone's coal bin in preparation for the next winter. From the sound of the coal hitting the chute, you could tell if it was lump coal or stoker coal. Stoker coal is ground-up coal and sounds like gravel when shoveled.

Let's remember the *Sounds of the Horace Mann School Complex*:

Our Janitor, Mr. Franklin, used to ring a large brass hand bell to call students to the classrooms in the morning, at noon and at the recesses. If you didn't get

116

into that building by the last vibration of the bell's last CLANG . . . it was a trip to Principal Van Cleve's office.

Cleaning the erasers from the blackboards also had a characteristic sound, as did the sound of the occasional fingernail being scraped down the blackboard. Of course there was also the sound of the John Philip Sousa marches as we marched out of the building at noon and at end of day.

When the High School track team was practicing at home, you could hear the crack of the starter's pistol and the thunk of the shot put hitting the ground.

The baseball team provided the crack of the baseball against the hickory or ash Louisville slugger bats. There were no aluminum bats then. There was also the PLUNKING sound of the ball hitting the catcher's mitt as the pitcher warmed up.

The football team supplied the sound of footballs being kicked and the crunching of leather pads during scrimmages.

Finally, one or two nights before the South/Central football game on Thanksgiving Day, there would always be a huge bonfire and pep rally in the center space of the running track. There you would also hear the cheerleaders and a loud Pep Band.

The *Sounds of Baxter's Woods*.

When we would climb the fence and walk towards Baxter's Woods, there always seemed to be an eerie stillness. But we would no sooner get into the woods than a blue jay would sound off and make us jump. He was warning the other blue jays and woods creatures of our approach.

117

A black crow would fly out of the top of a dead tree and make the sound of CAW...CAW...CAW. When you got near a grove of hickories or oaks you would hear the tch..tch...tch of a fox squirrel scolding us. In the distance you might hear the cackle of a rooster pheasant.

Sometimes as you walked along silently on a carpet of fallen leaves and twigs, a covey of quail would explode from beneath your feet and scare the dickens out of you.

Not to be forgotten were the sounds encountered down *at Russell's Point Amusement Park at Indian Lake*.

As you walked along the boat docks at the entrance to the park, there were six or eight sleek, polished inboard motorboats, their Chris Craft engines idling and producing a throaty, gurgling sound. They would take you on a ride for a dollar. Idling out, you'd hear the water lapping against the boat. Then, when they would "open 'er up," the roar was deafening and you usually got soaked from the spray – but, it was fun.

Back on land, you would proceed to the midway and hear the calliope on the merry-go-round. Or, further down, you'd hear a barker urging you to show your skill and win a beautiful prize by being able to knock down some bottles within three pitches.

As you approached the roller coaster, you could hear the riders being belted into their cars. Then the train of cars would begin to move slowly and start up the greatest pinnacle. As it slowly moved up, you could hear the clink...clink...clink of the chain pulling the car up to the top and then you would hear a "WHOOSSHHH" amid cries and screams of fear and

118

joy. The rides only lasted 2 minutes or so and you'd then hear the click...click ...click of the returning cars with their cargo of scared occupants.

Other memories:

I can still recall the hoof beats of the pacers and trotters at the Allen County Fair and the "RINGGG" of hammers on iron at the blacksmith shop. Perhaps I should save these for another story.

Since I have matured and have acquired "AIDS" (hearing aids that is), I am ever so grateful that I can remember those sounds of growing up. As wonderful as my hearing aids are, the sounds I can hear leave something to be desired when compared to the sounds I used to hear!

21.   Bums, Hobos and Knights of the Open Road

I learned a lot about the economy and the human condition just by looking around me as I grew up during the 1930's.

Our house was only three blocks from the Pennsylvania Railroad's main line from Chicago to New York. That area also contained the switch yards where freight trains would drop off coal cars and boxcars for our local markets.

As you may recall, back in the days of Robin Hood, the serfs were not allowed to chop down any trees. But whatever branches and limbs fell to the ground in a windstorm were considered "windfall" and fair game for whoever found it.

Back during the depression, coal cars sitting on a siding were also vulnerable to "windfall." Under the cover of darkness, someone would get up and help those loose coal pieces fall off the car as his neighbors would gather them up in a gunny sack (today called a burlap bag). My older brother once got a "scutching" [whipping] for remarking to visitors that we burn "hand-picked" coal. (For those not familiar, the term I used is an expression that comes from the old "scutching" paddle, a wide flat paddle used in making flax into thread so it could be used on a spinning wheel.)

Well now, times were hard, and since we were only three blocks from the railroad, we got frequent callers at our back door.

At this time, I need to define some terms:

1. A *bum* is an idle or good-for-nothing person, often drunk, and not prone to work for a reward.

but!

2. A *tramp* or hobo, by contrast, is a person who travels from place to place, doing odd jobs for food and lodging. Some were considered migratory workers before the term was coined later on.

Rev. Welty, down at the Lima Rescue Home, which was located near three railroads, referred to his clients as "transients" or "itinerants." His place was known far and wide in the hobo and tramp circles. They knew that, if they had 25 cents, they would get a room if they would get cleaned up with the soap he would give them and sit through a chapel service. They would even get supper, if they did it all. It was known as "Soup, Soap, and Salvation."

As I was saying, since we lived so close to the railroad, we got frequent knocks on the back door. Like all kids, I was eager to answer the knocks. Some poor hobo, with his hat in his hand, would ask if my mother was home. I would tell Mom that we had another one at the back door and she would come and listen to his sad tale of woe.

In the spring, they would offer to spade the garden or do any other odd jobs that she needed done. I never saw her turn anyone away. She would give the man a basin of warm water to wash his hands and face as she prepared a plate for him, and she invariably gave him a cup of coffee.

121

Very few of these fellas looked tough or evil, but more like poor Joes who were down on their luck. If they asked anything about lodgings, Mom would give them directions to the rescue home.

Our old dog, Queen, would lie in our neighbor's back yard and bark as a tramp was walking up our driveway to the back door. Thus, she always actually *directed* them to our back door, and then she would lie there and wag her tail.

As kids, we would play at the first and second railroad culverts. The second culvert had a little woods and a good sledding hill and skating pond. There was also a hobo camp there, and if any of the hobos were in camp, we would go over and talk to them. Often, they would be making mulligan stew in a No. 10 tomato can over a wood fire. We weren't afraid and I can't ever remember a kid's being harmed by a tramp.

In that ten-year period, from 1930 to 1940, we had plenty of hobos. I can remember being in our car at a railroad crossing when a slow freight was moving through town, and many of the boxcars with open doors would have a hobo standing in the door looking out. We found out that the hobos looked out for one another and they all carried chalk. They had code signs that they put on telephone poles and on curbs to signify good houses, bad houses, bad dogs etc.

Pearl Harbor signaled the beginning of the end of Hoboism.

Another term I should enlarge upon is the "Knights of the Open Road." This referred to the hitchhikers along the highways. I confess to having been a member in good standing of the Knighthood. After I entered college in Columbus, Ohio, I would hitchhike home on Fridays, and back to Columbus on Sunday. Mom would take me out to the east side of town on Route 309 and I would position myself on the highway to allow enough slowing-down time for a driver to be able to pull over and pick me up. Then I would stick out my thumb while Mom watched from her car. I would get a ride in short order and I would see Mom turning and leaving for home as I got into my ride. Sometimes, it would take me three or four rides to get home and sometimes I would get a single ride all the way.

When I got into ROTC, I was issued a regulation Army uniform with blue lapels. When I wore that to hitchhike, it was a snap getting rides. The drivers all wanted to know about the unusual uniform and I always acted very secretive about it and told them it was Special Forces and I wasn't allowed to talk about it.

After the war, it was still pretty easy to get rides. In fact, in 1948 I went home to buy a used car so that I could readily get from the hospital, where I lived, to the University. Just past Marysville, I saw a guy in a Navy flight jacket standing by the road with his thumb out. I picked him up and we chatted as I drove along. He said that he as going to enter medical school at Ohio State. "What a coincidence," I said, "so am I."

As it turned out, Bill Grannis and I signed in together, drew the same cadaver for anatomy, joined the same medical fraternity, graduated together, and

123

interned at the same hospital for a year. We then joined together, built an office, and practiced together for 20 years.

- - -

I think Bing Crosby summed up this whole era in two songs he recorded: "Brother, Can You Spare a Dime?" and "Going My Way?"

22. Our Entertainment Indoors

Someone asked me why I chose to write about entertainment during this time period (1930 -1940), and it was for several reasons.

1) Recreation between age five to age fifteen occupied a ten-year chunk of my life, during which a great deal of my education took place -- both in the classrooms and outside -- in the social graces of forming friendships and relationships, and

2) There was NO television, and we had to listen to broadcasts and learn to form pictures in our heads from the words, and many of those pictures are still in my mind.

Entertainment was in two forms: indoor and outdoor. I think I will break this account into two stories, and this first story will be about the way we entertained ourselves when it was raining outside or it was too hot, too cold, or dark outside.

A) CARD GAMES:
We had numerous card games to play. I will not go into the rules and manner of play of each game, but will simply name the games we played:
1. Whist
2. Old Maid
3. Crazy Eights
4. Hearts
5. 500 Rum

B) BOARD GAMES were popular, and there were a multitude, but I will only name the ones I myself played:

1. *Monopoly* is to me the all-time winner of the board games. In addition to being fun, it taught money management at an early age.
2. Parcheesi
3. Battleship. We would make our own cards, but now one can buy pre-printed cards.
4. Old Maid
5. Checkers. My pal, Eldon, used to beat me three out of four games. (I don't think I ever played a game of chess.)
6. Chinese checkers, played with marbles on a special board.
7. Crossword puzzles
8. Jigsaw puzzles

Speaking of puzzles, my mother had a great liking for jigsaw puzzles, and the harder, the better. She'd borrow them from neighbors and lend hers out. Our neighbor to the east, Blanche Anderson, thought that jigsaw puzzles were a tool of the Devil and, if you worked them, you were bound to end up in Hades playing jigsaw puzzles for the rest of eternity, and all of the puzzles would have three or four non-contiguous pieces missing. (I don't mean to malign Blanche, for she was a sweet woman. Before I went overseas, she called me to her house and told me to always remember Joshua 1:9, and it would guide me and comfort me.)

C) RADIO! -- it became the staple of the household as much as TV and computers have become so today. Let me go through a typical day of radio in our house when I was growing up.

126

Morning
7:00 AM   WOWO, Ft. Wayne.
Rev. E. Howard Cadle and his wife, Mother Cadle, who would do the singing (example:"Ere you left your room this morning, did you think to pray?").
8:00 AM   WLS, Chicago, featured troubadours and balladeers like Bradley Kincaid and Burl Ives.
9:00 AM   Cliff Roberson, a comedian who used to sing the news and start out by singing, "I see by the paper . . ." and then he would sing the news item.
10:00 till Noon   WLS, Chicago -- Livestock and crop reports

Afternoon
WLW, Cincinnati
          The *original* soaps:
"Ma Perkins," sponsored by Oxydol;
"Stella Dallas," sponsored by Rinso followed by
"When A Girl Marries," sponsored by Proctor
          and Gamble
4:00 PM   Kids were home from school, so there would be all the kids stories and shows: First: "Jack Armstrong, the All-American Boy," sponsored by Wheaties
4:30 PM   "Don Winslow of the Navy."
5:00 PM   "Orphan Annie" and her famous code ring, sponsored by Ovaltine.
5:30 PM   "The Lone Ranger" and Tonto.
6:00 to 7:00 PM   Supper time – "Lowell Thomas."

Evening
7:00 PM   "Amos and Andy"
7:30 PM   "Lum and Abner"
8:00 PM   Jack Benny, then

127

Fred Allen, then
"Fibber McGee and Molly," then
"The Bickersons" with Don Ameche
and Frances Langford.
On Sunday night, when Walter Winchell was on, there
was also "One Man's Family," a serial that Mom
absolutely would not miss.

10:00 PM the Longines/Wittenauer program of
classical music

11:00 PM WLW -- you could get Peter Grant with
"Moon River," and drift off to sleep ready to start
tomorrow.

D) SPECIALTY RADIO –

SPORTING EVENTS.

1) *Football games* --We would get Ohio State and
   Notre Dame games. We would get the Rose
   Bowl on New Years Day and a description of
   the Rose Parade preceding the game.

2) *Baseball games* -- play by play, ticker-tape type
   of description of the Detroit Tigers, the
   Cleveland Indians and the Cincinnati Reds, and
   the World Series, play-by-play, in late
   September.

3) In May we would get the description of the
   Kentucky Derby.

4) *Boxing* -- Ringside narrations of all the big-time
   boxing events. Neighbors would gather around
   the best radio set on the block to listen to the
   blow-by-blow description of the greatest
   champion of our era, the "Bronze Bomber," Joe
   Louis, from Detroit, when he destroyed Max
   Schmeling, the German challenger.

128

5) There were many stars: Jack Dempsey, Billy Conn, Rocky Graziano, and many of the Caribbean fly weights, bantam weights, etc.

SERIAL AND MYSTERY SHOWS.

1) *The G-Men* -- they always had a "Most Wanted" list, and John Dillnger and Harry Pierpont made it for weeks at a time until Dillinger was apprehended in Chicago, "betrayed by the Lady in Red."

2) *The Green Hornet*

3) *"Only 'The Shadow' Knows."* My older brother, Ken, had a nasty habit of listening from the darkened kitchen while we were all in the living room. He would sneak out the back door, come round the house, sneak up on the front porch and, just at the climax of the suspense, he would *RAP LOUDLY!* on the big glass window, and Mom and I would jump up to the ceiling and have to be helped off the chandelier.

THE GRAND CHAMPION.

For me, the Grand Champion of all radio events only happened every four years, when I would get a double-dose of the *Democratic* and *Republican National Conventions*.

Lima, Ohio gained national attention one year when Francis Durbin, a local delegate to the Democratic convention, gave one of the "seconding speeches" for Franklin Delano Roosevelt.

These conventions were great because the commentators would paint word pictures of all the events, such as the release of balloons, and the

129

various state delegations as they marched and demonstrated, touting their favorite sons.

The roll call of the states, and other convention business, was never broadcast until 5 or 6 PM, and it lasted until early in the morning. It was summer and there was no school, and I could stay up as late as I wanted to listen to the roll calls, vote counts, delegates' remarks, and the brass bands.

We really got schooled in Robert's Rules of Order!

They finished in the early mornings, due to the activities in the smoke-filled rooms. You would hear how there was a smell of cigar smoke with a tinge of bourbon; two of the most active men there were Mr. Jack Daniels and Mr. Jim Beam.

To run that convention from the podium was very stressful and I think they did it in shifts. They had to have accurate accountants to tally the votes from the polling by the delegates.

Frequently, early in the convention there would be four or five candidates, but by Friday afternoon, after all the jaw-boning, and parading, and polling -- and the frequent delegations to and conferring with Misters Daniels and Beam -- the convention would agree on a single candidate. Then came the acceptance speeches of the presidential nominee and the vice-presidential nominee.

I always thought it quite odd that Mr. Daniels and Mr. Beam never got any recognition in the press at home, and their pictures never appeared in the hometown papers.

23. Aunt Lydia and Uncle Ray

As I look back, I don't know if I really should pick out a favorite aunt or uncle, even though I did earlier in the book. They were all unique, and thoroughly enjoyable. Actually, I can't think of any uncle or aunt that I didn't like.

Now, Aunt Lydia and Uncle Ray Murray, for example, were a perfectly matched couple. They were both very outgoing and each had a great sense of humor. Even as a child, I greatly enjoyed talking to them. For brevity's sake, I will refer to Aunt Lydia as Liddy and Uncle Ray as Ray, which are the names that Mom and Dad used when speaking of them. This is certainly not meant as any disrespect, for I loved them dearly.

When we would arrive at their home or they came to ours, as soon as the adults greeted each other, Liddy would stoop down to my eye level and greet me personally with a big smile and a hug and small talk befitting a young boy. Liddy loved jokes of all kinds and kept a little black book of key words and phrases and punch lines to help her remember her favorite stories. She had a roof-shaking laugh and after I had reached adult status, whenever she would greet me, she would ask if I had any good stories for her.

I believe Ray and Liddy lived in half of a double house on North Charles Street. Liddy's sister and mother, Cora Fisher and Mrs. Beery, respectively, lived in the other half. Her sister, Cora, was the widow of Fred Fisher, an attorney who left her fairly well-fixed. Liddy's mother was somewhat of a naturopath and kept a "divining rod" or "stick". She had many

131

home remedies for treating her friends who would come for her ministrations.

Ray worked in a hardware store called "Evans and Thomas" on the west side of Main Street in Lima, just a few doors north of the courthouse. When I was about three years old, I once visited that store where Ray worked and, as I remember, a small tricycle caught my eye. I think that is where Santa Claus later found it and moved it from to under our Christmas tree.

The hardware store was later sold to Fred Drescher, who ran it for awhile, and who later sold it to Longmeier and Stippich. At this point, the store moved across Main to the east side of the street and gradually became Stippich's Hardware. It was later taken over by the American House Restoration and it is their building today.

Somewhere in all these ownership changes, Ray left the hardware business and started working for a roofing company that was doing a big job out at the Solar Refinery in Lima.

It was in the summertime when it was beastly hot and, as coincidence would have it, John Stuber, a later-made family friend who surprised us with this story, was the foreman for Carey Roofers on that job. When the job was finished, the contractor had a party for the workers and supplied free beer and sandwiches. I suspect that they had some other kinds of spirits floating around, too. As the story was told to me, Ray got "bombed," and they didn't know what to do with him. So, John Stuber and the others took him home and told Aunt Liddy that he had gotten "gassed" at the refinery, but that he would be OK in the morning.

After the roofing job was completed in Lima, Ray and Liddy moved to Bellefontaine. They had a house on the main thoroughfare and, since their daughter, Ellen, had left for Nursing School at Grant Hospital in Columbus, her folks rented her room out to an old bachelor.

At that time, Uncle Ray drove a gasoline truck and delivered fuel to the farmers. As he drove around, he would have access to many farms that came up for sale and, after some years, he and Liddy purchased a large farm in Bellefontaine, near the highest point in the state of Ohio. It had both a good main house and a good tenant house. It also had a good barn, and a sugar camp in its extensive woods, with a thousand oaken buckets.

Meanwhile, cousin Ellen married and she and her husband moved into the tenant house. Ray was a good farmer and had a huge team of Belgian horses, and each horse weighed over a ton. Ray was only about 5 feet 7 inches tall and weighed about 145 pounds, so he had to stand on a box to throw the harness over them. He was so proud of that team of horses!

Ray raised good purebred livestock, such as Hereford cattle, Shropshire sheep, and Duroc hogs. Liddy was a bit more egalitarian, with her flock of chickens. She had a few each of Barred Rocks, Rhode Island Reds, Plymouth Rocks and Leghorns. She was a very hard worker and her fruit and root cellar was a sight to behold.

When they butchered a beef, she would put up corned beef in both huge and smaller-size mason jars. Whenever company popped in unexpectedly, she had beef, pork, chicken and sausage all preserved, as well

133

as corn, beans, beets, pickles, pumpkin, pears, peaches, cherries and a well-stocked freezer with ice cream and more. It was quite a long way to town, so she was always prepared.

Liddy loved to have company, so in March of my senior year in medical school, she invited Polly, Scotty (who was just 2 months old) and me to Sunday dinner. We were to drive there from Columbus, and she also invited Mom, Dad, and my brother, Kenneth, to drive down from Lima.

We all met at the farm and Liddy was in her glory with a new baby to hold and fuss over. She handed Scott to my brother, Ken, for a picture and it was the first time he had held Scott. Scotty looked up at Uncle Ken, smiled, and then loudly loaded his diaper. Ken hastily handed him back to Polly like Dan Marino handing off a football to a running back. I thought Aunt Liddy would burst, she laughed so hard!

During my internship, Polly, Scott and I lived on a farm that Mom and Dad had bought and were then inhabiting. We got interested in livestock and bought a heifer from Uncle Ray. We didn't know it, and Ray said he didn't know it, either, but our heifer, "Hildegarde," had been impregnated and was with calf.

So at the end of the gestation period, we got a bonus, and then we owned *two* cows! With the pressure of starting my practice, I didn't have time for the cows and Polly was busy with Scott and Robin, who had come along, so we sold them to Dad, and he later sold them at auction.

Dad and Uncle Ray were always a sketch to be around. They would taunt and tease each other. Ray was a died in the wool Democrat and Dad, for the sake of argument, became an ardent Republican. Dad used to call Uncle Ray "Rochester" who was Jack Benny's butler, and that would start things rolling. It was always in good fun and they never offended each other and always parted with an embrace. For a long time, Ray was known as "Uncle Rochester" when we spoke of him at home.

Some time later, hard work and time caught up with Liddy, and she died rather abruptly of what seemed to be a cardiac death.

After Aunt Liddy's passing, Uncle Ray just lost his starch and his desire. I think he sold the farm to his grandson, Ellen's only child, and moved to a nursing home, as he had advanced prostatic cancer. He passed away there and went to join Aunt Lydia.

My Dad, and my brother, Ken, and I used to hunt rabbits on Uncle Ray's farm. The old sugar camp was never used and the wooden buckets just rotted away. We used to joke about Uncle Ray getting "gassed " at the refinery, but I don't believe Aunt Lydia ever really bought that story. She was too bright a star to have that sheep farmer pull the wool over her eyes.

Uncle Ray (left)
and Dad (right)

24.   The Clothes We Wore

This subject really requires the stretching of my memory to over sixty years ago. I'll try to bring some vignettes up for view, progressing from youngsters, to teenagers, to adults.

BOYS: I've opted to start with boys because I remember best what I wore ---not to say, however, that I didn't notice or pay any attention to the girls. As I remember, in some of my early Adon Studio portraits, I was dressed up for viewing, not for playing.

One of the items of clothing I remember best was my lace-up leather boots, which came to just below my knees. This type and style of boot became my favorite shoe to wear in the great outdoors. I think I wore them from about ages six to ten, when new ones needed to be purchased as I continued to grow. My prize possession was the knife in the little pocket on the outside of the right leg. These boots were my pride and joy and I used to water-proof them with "dubbing,"   a Vaseline-like product used for the purpose.

With the boots, I wore long wool hunting socks with red or green piping around the tops. With those boots, I also generally wore knickers (short for "Knickerbockers") of "canvas duck" or corduroy. If I were going out in the snow or woods to hunt or play, I would wear a flannel shirt or a Woolrich green-and-black-checkered shirt. For wear in less cold weather, I would put on ankle-high leather shoes with heavy socks and knickers or Oshkosh B'gosh denim pants.

I think that about every boy from about ages seven to ten, at one time or another, owned an aviator's leather helmet with a pair of goggles. It covered the ears from frost bite and fastened with a snap under the chin.

For grade school, most boys wore Oxford shoes with long socks and knickers, a long-sleeved shirt and a sweater. For dress up occasions, a pre-tied tie on an elastic band with a hook fastener would secure the collar. For really sloppy weather, we wore "four-buckle arctics" (boots) over our shoes.

In Junior High, our outfits were mostly long pants of cotton, wool, or corduroy, with a shirt and sweater. Gym class required a pair of Keds (black), shorts with elastic around the top, and a tank top.

In High School, it was more of the same, but possibly with saddle shoes or penny loafers or wing tip Oxfords. Mom got me a 3/4 length leather top coat which was very sharp. I never owned a sport coat until I got invited to a Sadie Hawkins dance. Mom found out about the invitation and took me down to Gregg's Department Store, bought me a coat that she liked, and made me go to the dance.

GIRLS: In grade school, girls wore long socks which always seemed to be falling down unless they wore elastic garters up above their knees. Usually, they wore one-piece dresses, and shoes with a strap and buckle across the top, with patent leathers for dress-up. If you get hold of a Norman Rockwell picture album, you will no doubt feel as I do that he was certainly the greatest illustrator of our time and depicted so well all the facets of our dress at work and play. In such a book I'm sure you would see a typical school girl from this time period in a dress, with pig-tail braids in her hair and falling stockings.

When girls went to Junior High, they graduated to skirts, blouses and sweaters and they still wore the same shoes. The one big change was what the girls wore for gym class: big, one-piece blue outfits called bloomers. Girls had white Keds and the boys wore black Keds.

In High School, the girls blossomed out with saddle shoes and penny loafers, and skirts with bobby sox, blouses, and sweaters. They sometimes wore the letter sweaters of their boyfriends or one of their own from cheerleading. They also acquired decorative rain coats and car coats -- slacks had not made the scene back then. Hair ribbons were "in" and so were hair clasps.

WOMEN: This category covers everyone from new moms, to those in middle age, to grandmothers. My mom always wore stockings and I don't remember seeing her with bare legs, ever! The usual outfit for housework was a dress with an apron.

For dressing up in the 30's, hats and gloves were in style. I remember that hats came in all shapes, colors, and sizes, from pill boxes to pork pies to wide-brimmed hats. Also in fashion were high heels and silk stockings with seams down the back. Mom was partial to the Enna Jetticks brand of women's shoes.

Cold weather outer wear ranged from warm wool coats to full-length furs. I remember that my mom had a nice coat with a beaver collar and when I was a little kid in the wintertime and she would scoop me up, I loved to bury my face in her coat collar which had snow flakes on it and smelled so good from her cologne!

Slacks and coveralls were not seen until around 1942 when women entered the work force and helped to arm the country to bring about the downfall of Germany, Italy and Japan.

MEN: The men I saw most often in the 30's wore heavy work shoes and socks and the most common working outfit was bib overalls from Oshkosh B'gosh. And from J.C. Penney's, Sears, and Montgomery Wards they would get Chambray blue work shirts and appropriate headgear such as a railroader's cap. I remember that my dad wore long underwear in the winter and BVD's (or, as we called them, "BBD's") in the summer, which were one-piece suits of underwear.

For dress-up back then, Nunn Bush black and white wing tips were the fashionable shoes. Trousers were sharply pressed, with a white shirt and an open collar and sleeves rolled up one or two turns on the forearm. Some men wore suspenders and some wore belts. A very popular dress item was a straw "boater" (hat) made by Mallory or Stetson. It had a wide brim all around and a rather flat crown. I think it was made in Panama.

The well-dressed man might have on a sport or suit coat and keep a pack of Beeman's pepsin gum or an envelope packet of Sen Sen in his pocket, and he might well smell like Aqua Velva aftershave lotion.

So this is the way things shaped up in the 30's, as best I recall, and these are the things I remember most vividly from those days.

25. Aunt Lu and Uncle Charlie, Revisited

Early on in my memoirs, I wrote a story about "A Tribute to Uncle Charlie". I talked about the family structure: Charlie, Lula, their daughter Roberta, and the six-year-old son they had lost to meningitis back before medicine had the benefit of antibiotics. Their son's death would have been a tragic loss to any family but was especially so for a farm family.

Aunt Lu was my mother's older, and only, sister. As I reread my tribute to Uncle Charlie, it became apparent to me that I hadn't recognized Aunt Lu enough for her contribution to this "Farm Family Team".

I grew up in town and all the farm experiences I gained and that I treasure today came from both Aunt Lu and Uncle Charlie. I'm sure that in their eyes, I was a surrogate for their lost son, Russell. What follows will be a potpourri, a pleasant mixture from my many farm experiences as I look back-- some painful, some amusing, but all in all, most vivid and pleasant. If I repeat myself from time to time, as we older storytellers are prone to do, just chalk it up to repeated reverie.

While Uncle Charlie ran the barn, the animals and the fields, Aunt Lu's domain was the house, the garden and the henhouse.

Aunt Lu was the Commander in Chief of the henhouse. All hens think that their job is to sit on a nest of eggs and produce chicks, but Aunt Lu had a different table of organization. Out of a flock of about thirty or forty Plymouth Rock hens (and four or five roosters), she would allow only four or five of the hens to sit and raise chicks. The remainder were the laborers who produced eggs for the table and for trading to the huckster for money or merchandise.

While the chickens did have their own "pecking order," of course, for the conduct of the flock, Aunt Lu was the final arbiter in the politics of the hen house. If a hen stopped laying and wasn't nesting, she became a candidate for the next chicken and dumpling meal.

Occasionally in the spring, a hen would wander off and set up a nest in the tall grass or in a brush pile and hatch a nest full of eggs. A fertilized egg hatches in about three weeks, so after about four to six weeks the wayward hen would lead her brood out and show them off. She made clucking noises to her chicks that told them when to come back to her if a rain storm was coming or a chicken hawk was circling overhead, and they would all scurry back and get under her protective wings.

Successful management of the henhouse assured a steady supply of eggs, fryers and stewing hens. I noted that Aunt Lu always talked to her chickens when she was working around them or in the hen house. I asked her why she talked to the chickens and she replied that "they are the only ones around here who don't jaw back at me!"

In addition to the chickens, she always had a little colony of guinea fowl or hens. They generally

143

kept to themselves and didn't require much care. They were quite skittish and easily frightened, which made them frequently produce characteristic loud, shrill cries of agitation whenever anything strange came into their area. Aunt Lu kept them as her "burglar alarms," much to the consternation of my cousin, Roberta, as they invariably announced her arrival home from a "late date."

The garden was a typical farm garden, with sweet corn, green beans, pickles, dill, sweet peas, potatoes, tomatoes, plus a rhubarb bed in the shade. By the house there were apple trees, pear trees, and an apricot tree. In the back, near the basement door, was the windmill for the pump, and it formed an arbor for the most delicious white grapes. They tasted so good on a hot August day! Straight out back from the house was the outhouse, complete with both Sears Roebuck and Montgomery Ward catalogs.

The house was a large one, with a front porch, a living room with a pump organ, a dining room, a large kitchen and a wash room for cleaning up and for hanging up work clothes. The basement was a cool place in the summer, and there they kept the eggs, milk and cream, along with canned goods and cured hams. The DeLaval milk separator was kept upstairs in the wash room.

The barn was Uncle Charlie's domain where he kept his beloved mules, Maude and Jack, and Robert, the old horse. There was a huge hay mow with chutes down to the feed boxes of the mules and horses, and also to the cows' stanchions where they fed as they were milked. I actually learned how to milk a cow there and had my head switched with a cow's tail many times while milking, depending on the fly population at the time.

There were several things I always looked forward to when I stayed up on the farm. One, as I told about previously, was when Aunt Lu and I would make homemade ice cream as a surprise for Uncle Charlie.

The other thing I always looked forward to was Friday, around noon, when the Huckster wagon would come from the general store. The huckster driver would take Aunt Lu's eggs and give her cash or merchandise: a spool of thread, or a tin of Cloverine Salve, or whatever else she saw that she wanted. Of course, he also carried penny candy, so I would go to my room and go through my pockets for some cash. Such hard decisions I had to make, as to which candies I would choose!

As I said in the beginning, this was to be a potpourri of experiences, mostly enjoyable, but some painful. I now want to relate a couple of the "painful" memories.

When I was about five years old, my parents, sister and I went up to the farm for a Sunday visit. I had taken my bathing suit along, as I thought there might be enough water in the drainage ditch to swim or splash around in. After dinner, I put on my bathing suit, and Roberta, my sister, Mary, and I went walking barefoot down the gravel roadway to where the ditch went under the road.

There was some water in the ditch at the bridge, so I ran ahead and started down through the weeds to the water's edge. Suddenly, I was engulfed by the worst stinging pains I had ever experienced! My arms and legs were instantly covered with burning, stinging welts and all I could do was squall and bawl!

My sister hoisted me up on her back and carried me back to the house where my folks were alarmed, as were with Uncle Charlie and Aunt Lu. They washed my arms and legs, and the cool water helped. Uncle Charlie diagnosed my problem as "horse nettles."

Needless to say, I have stayed away from unknown weeds ever since. But, about fifty years later, we were living on South Cole Street and we had a couple of half-barrels with flowers in them. I noticed a slim green weed sticking up through the mulch of one, so I reached down and picked it out. As soon as I touched it, the nettle sting hit me! And my memory went racing back to that ditch of long ago.

Another less painful and more humorous experience happened when Uncle Charlie and I were "haying it." I was driving the mules and Uncle Charlie was taking the hay with his pitchfork as it came up the hay loader, and distributing it evenly over the wagon.

We kept moving forward and had almost a full load when a big bunch of Canadian thistles came up from the loader. Uncle Charlie pitched them up and they happened to fall right behind me. Right about then the wagon hit a rut and I fell backward, sitting down hard right on top of the thistles! I was rather painfully surprised and shouted out in a loud voice, "Merry *Christmas!*" This so amused Uncle Charlie that he almost fell off the hay load laughing.

I'm sure that had Uncle Charlie not been there I would have burst forth with some choice playground profanity. But Uncle Charlie went on to relate the incident to Aunt Lu and my folks, and it became an oft-told yarn for many years at family gatherings.

Well, the potpourri has come to an end. I'll never forget the stinging nettles or the pillow of thistles. But the wonderful memories of making hay, harvesting wheat and oats, de-tasseling hybrid corn, gathering eggs with Aunt Lu, hearing the guinea hen cries, driving the mules and milking the cows will never leave me. To be a partner on a farm team like that was exhilarating for this city boy. I liked that place so much that I once rode alone on my bike 25 miles from Lima to get there, but that is a story for another time.

26. Outdoor Entertainment

Our "outside entertainment" sometimes took place away from the neighborhood and occasionally some far distance from home, like at a Boy Scout Camp, Church Camp or at Russell's Point Amusement Park.

To define our "neighborhood" itself; it was more than just the nearby households, and included the entire Horace Mann school and recreational area. This actually took up ten acres square, or about 8 city blocks.   The local areas that were out of the neighborhood that we frequented included Faurot Park, Baxter's Woods, the downtown movie houses, and the roller skating rink.

Of course we didn't have Nintendos or any other electronic entertainment. In fact, pinball machines first started to appear in the early 1940's. Many times after a tag football game we would ride our bikes down to Yoestings Bakery to get a large ice-cold Pepsi in a glass bottle and a glazed donut, and play the pinball machine once or twice.

The games we played around our homes, mostly in the evenings after supper (if our homework was done), were as follows:

Our *sidewalk and front step games.* were those such as Red Light/Green Light, Simon Says, Mother May I, Hop Scotch and jacks.

(It was fun back then. . . .)

Yard games were such as Over the Mountain, Red Rover, Hide and Go Seek, and Statues. In the Statues game, the "it" person would grab a person from the circle by the wrist and start swinging that person in a circular path until there was enough centrifugal force. Then he would let go of the wrist and the person would fly head-over-heels into the grass and then had to maintain the position he ended in as a "statue." When all the players had been "statue-ized," the swinger would walk around and judge everyone for the originality of their statuesque positions and then pick the winner, who would become "it" and repeat the process.

(Yes, it was fun back then!)

In the spring, when the warm breezes began to blow, young boys' thoughts turned not to love but to kites. Many guys made their own triangular kites, and some would get plans out of *Popular Mechanics* and make a box kite. I only tried it once and it worked OK! The box kites didn't need a tail and they looked like toady's "Space Labs" up in the sky.

The triangular kites always needed a tail for either balance or ballast (depending on wind speed), and it would become quite a trial-and-error job to get the right length of tail to keep the kite from nose-diving into the giant elm tree on the Horace Mann lot. That was the original "kite-eating tree" of Charlie Brown, and, throughout the year, one could see numerous kites in various states of digestion in that kite-eating elm tree.

(Boy, it was fun back then. . .)

In Fall and Winter, our games would vary in location. Touch football, kick the can and roller skating

149

would take place on the smooth asphalt of College Avenue. Basketball would be in Bob Creviston's back yard. There would be pep rallies, snake dances, and bonfires on the college grounds before the South/Central game. October and November saw nut- and bittersweet-gathering in the woods.

Come winter, we had lasting snows -- seems like we used to have snow on the ground for longer periods than nowadays. Over in the playground area, we'd make a huge wheel in the snow with spokes and a hub in the center to play "Fox and Geese." We'd also make snow forts and igloos and have snowball fights. Lots of energy was burned and everyone went home with rosy cheeks.

One day, I had just jumped off my porch onto the snowy yard when -- *POW!* -- Bob Creviston popped me with a big, wet snowball. So I grabbed some snow and plopped it in his face and he started chasing me. I slipped and fell on my back in my front yard and Bob was coming after me, and just as he was about to smother me with snow, I raised my icy, muddy boot and got him "right in the mush" (in the face)! He recoiled and started squalling, and went bawling home.

And I knew I was in trouble. I crawled behind the front shrubs, against our front porch wall, and huddled down. Just then, I looked up and saw the mailman, Mr. Hover. He had a grin on his face and he said, "I saw you get him, but he had it coming. I won't tell anyone where you are hiding." And he chuckled as he continued on his way.

Nothing came of it. I think Bob's mom and mine probably figured that we had settled things. The next day we were pals again.

It seems that every neighborhood (we referred to our turf as a neighborhood and we never became a "gang") has at least one special "character" or unusual individual who stands out. We had one such person, a girl who could have become "Miss Tomboy of Ohio." She lived south of me at the far end of College Avenue. She was a pleasant, thin (even skinny) girl with a bit of an overbite, and freckles. Whoever won the "bat toss" for choosing up sides for a ball game would always choose Norlene Guthrie first. She had the best under-arm fastball pitch I ever saw, and she could hit and field well wherever she played. She was always a fantastic tennis player and always won her class. We wouldn't let her play football with us because we didn't want her to get hurt -- or to show us up!

On another note, I have fond memories of a certain time one summer when it was miserably hot. My pal, Jack Lytle, and I decided to become entrepreneurs. Back in the early 1930's, the WPA was putting in new sewers along Hazel and College Avenues. Jack and I each got our two-gallon thermos bottles and made fresh lemonade. We went up and down the construction line hawking our wares. We only charged five cents a glass but I think those guys still always talked us into a bigger glass or a free refill. We had to be careful because the foreman on the job didn't like us taking up time with his laborers.

(No doubt about it: it was fun back then.)

During any and all seasons of the year, we used to play Cowboys and Indians or cops and robbers with cap guns. One thing we were careful not to let slip at the supper table was anything about our using BB guns in our fights. Such talk would have meant immediate confiscation of my copper-colored Red Ryder carbine BB gun. Every time I picked up that gun, I got the same lecture about the little boy in another neighborhood who had his eye put out with a BB.

We would go out to the "second culvert" on the edge of Baxter's Woods and choose up sides and make solemn promises not to shoot above the waist. We all had so many clothes on that it didn't hurt when you got shot. Fortunately, these games never lasted very long and no one ever got hurt. But it wasn't too smart, as I think about it, looking back.

(Still, it was fun back then!)

27. Holidays the Way I Remember Them

Our celebration of holidays in the 30's was somewhat subdued compared to today. We didn't have the wherewithal for expensive festivities, but we were thankful for what we did have. I don't think any of us thought of ourselves as being "poor." Things were grim at times, but our family and neighbors had the necessities of life and no one went hungry.

New Year's Day was, of course, a national holiday. Those who had celebrated too much prior to and after the stroke of midnight spent New Year's Day "recovering." There was no TV but I used to listen to the Rose Bowl game on the radio each year and we would have a scrumptious meal.

The Presidents Days, Lincoln on February 12 and Washington on February 22, were each celebrated in school on the appropriate days with readings and stories. No vengeful, venomous, *avant-garde* historians, college professors or media miscreants had come forward to denigrate these two of our great Presidents. But time has altered that!

St. Patrick's Day (March 17) was not a national holiday but was celebrated by the Irish in the North and South ends of Lima. The celebrations seemed to increase after 1933 and the repeal of Prohibition.

April holidays, other than the 1st day of April, were mostly near the end of the month and consisted of Palm Sunday, Good Friday, and Easter Sunday. My mom used to color hard-boiled eggs and hide them about our yard and shrubbery on the night before Easter. The next morning we would search for the treasures before Sunday school and church. The last thing to be found was a large Easter basket with the artificial green grass and chocolate-covered marshmallow chicks and bunnies and chocolate-filled eggs. Then it was off to Sunday school and church after breakfast and changing into our good clothes.

May Day. On the first day of May, the elementary schools would have a May Pole for the graduating sixth graders who would be going to Junior High in the fall.

Mother's Day. We would all give Mom a card (frequently made in art class) plus a gift which, most often, she didn't need except for the thought. She was always most gracious. Dad would generally take all of us to Jack's Cafeteria (formerly Jack and Yoshi's) for a chop suey dinner.

Toward the end of May would come Memorial Day. But back then we called it "Decoration Day," as that was when families would decorate the family graves in the cemeteries with flowers and, if they were Veterans' grave, with flags. There was generally a parade down Main Street with the American Legion Drum and Bugle Corps performing, along with high school bands. I remember seeing veterans of the Spanish-American War and World War I in those parades. Memorial Day signaled the beginning of summer fashions and it was thereafter proper to wear white clothes, accessories and shoes.

June. June 17 was Flag Day and everyone flew their flags at home, and all the downtown stores had flags out in front.

July. Independence Day, July the Fourth, was a *big day* of celebration, usually beginning with a parade downtown in the morning. There were no large firework displays at night as there are today. Instead, everyone tended to create their own displays. Starting early in the morning, you could smell the characteristic, pleasant aroma of burning punk sticks that were used to ignite firecrackers, etc. All day long you could hear the explosions of ladyfingers, cap pistols, two-inchers and cherry bombs.

Unfortunately, many people got injured shooting off the noisemakers. Bob Creviston, on one occasion, lit a two-incher and threw it. It didn't go off so he walked over and picked it up. THEN it went off and burned his hand. His folks were frightened that he might have damaged his fingers and wouldn't be able to play the piano, but he lucked out, a sadder but wiser celebrant.

In the evening, out came the sparklers, flower pots, Roman candles and sky rockets. Most parents were glad when the day was over. A family by the name of Katterheinrich on the corner of Rice and Jameson always had their front porch loaded with fireworks for sale from about the twentieth of June till July fifth.

August. August 18 was a very important day, but no one except me celebrated it, as it was my birthday.

September. The first Monday of September, Labor Day, always signaled the end of summer. The adults would put away their white shoes, pants and accessories. There was generally another parade, and school would start several days thereafter.

October. Our Halloween, October 31st, was just devilment most of the time (soaped windows and upset porch furniture). But in the late thirties "trick or treat" was started and took the vandalism out of the act.

November. The South/Central football game was a highlight of Thanksgiving Day (fourth Thursday in November). It was held at the old College Grounds until Lima Stadium was completed. It seemed always quite cold and everyone stomped home on cold feet to the awaiting Thanksgiving feast. The meal was sometimes pheasant and rabbit, and not always turkey. One time, Mom fixed a goose, but that was the last time because there was fat all over the oven and kitchen.

December. Christmas Eve was always beautiful, as our tree had already been decorated for a week or more. I would be hustled off to bed early, only to lie there awake in the greatest insomnia of anticipation. When I got up, I always found my stocking with several small lumps of coal, a potato and an orange or a tangerine. This had been the customary filling for stockings as far back as my dad's childhood. Sometimes the orange in the stocking was all the previous generation would get for Christmas. For us, I suppose the coal lumps and potato were meant as a sort of reminder of the hard times of the past. Anyway, after the stocking, Mom would start pulling packages from under the tree.

That afternoon, Bob Creviston and Jack Lytle would come to see what I had received and then I would go off to survey their loot, too. Christmas dinner was always great, with turkey or chicken, candied sweet potatoes, corn, scalloped potatoes and a date-nut roll that Mom had prepared the day before.

- - -

One Christmas I will never forget was when I was 10 years old. As we were unwrapping gifts, I received an envelope from my brother, Marvin, who was 20 years old and very much my senior. The note inside outlined a treasure hunt for my present.

The first clue said to look in the coldest place in the house for the next clue. I went to the Norge Refrigerator and in the ice cube compartment, I found an oblong package and a note. I ripped off the paper and there was the fore-piece for a shotgun! So I had some idea of what was coming!

The next clue was to look in a warm place in the house, so I had many places to look. Behind the gas burner in the living room fireplace I found the butt of an H&R single-shot gun.

The next clue was to look where Mom kept her "discipline stick," which was a broad yardstick standing in the corner behind the door to the back porch. There, I found the completion of my treasure

157

hunt -- and what a treasure it was: a little 20-gauge single-shot Harrington and Richards shotgun! I don't believe I could count the hours of pleasure I spent carrying that Christmas present around in the crook of my arm on my many hunting expeditions. Marvin had come through with the most memorable Christmas gift of my youth.

I passed his treasure hunt idea down in our family when I made one with a sand and beach theme for my daughter, Cindy's, birthday one year when we were vacationing in Sarasota. And others in the family have liked and used the idea, too.

Marvin was to look after me in many other ways as well: He arranged for extensive dental work I needed when I was eleven, and he helped me outline my education. He taught me the very entertaining hobby of filling balloons with hydrogen by snapping an empty balloon over the mouth of a pop bottle containing his magic ingredients. The balloon would fill with the pressure and could then be tied off. It could then be released to float up in the sky . . . Sometimes we would take one out into a deserted field with no wind, tie a paper tail to the balloon, light it, and watch as the balloon soared aloft, only to explode with a giant *BOOM!*

As you will later see, Marvin's insistence that I go to college may have literally saved my life!

And furthermore. when I got out of the service and went into pre-med, he gave me his very nice Bunsen burner from college for good luck. He introduced me to classical music with two great 45-rpm collections of the day, *The Heart of the Symphony*

158

and *The Heart of the Violin Concerto,* as well as an album of Chopin's ballet for orchestra *Les Sylphides.* And when I graduated medical school, he hosted a cocktail party for me in Oak Ridge where he then lived and, in a startling and dramatic toast I will never forget, hailed me as "the White Hope of the Murray family"!

You can imagine the effect this had on me, to receive such a powerful public compliment from an older brother I admired and respected so much! Marvin always held a special place in my heart. We always called him "Mark" and Polly and I gave our second son the middle name of Mark in tribute to Marvin.

- - -

Well now, perhaps we had best be getting back to the parade of the holidays. One week after Christmas would come <u>New Year's Eve</u>. The movie houses would run triple-headers and there was lots going on. There was no TV for watching the Ball coming down in Times Square, but we did have the music of Guy Lombardo and his Royal Canadians. And so, excuse me as I take my leave, for this is where I came in . . .

28. Some Smells and Tastes from A Bygone Time

Way back 65 or 70 years ago when I was growing up, life was much simpler, it seems to me, than the life I experience today. And yet, every now and then, I will encounter an aroma (I decline to use the word "odor," as that seems to have a negative connotation) or a taste that takes me back to my childhood.

Simple things . . .

The Barr Hotel bakery truck that used to come around once or twice a week was a veritable storehouse of smells and tastes. When the driver would swing those back doors open, a heavenly aroma would greet you. The slightly greasy smell of glazed donuts was intoxicating, as was the smell of the filled jellyrolls and chocolate-covered Bismarcks. The apple cinnamon pie would stake out its own position. And the breads! -- rye, whole wheat and especially "salt rising bread." (I could never get enough of salt rising bread and butter!)

But our whole neighborhood was a treasure trove of other smells and tastes, some pleasant and others not so pleasant, depending on the wind and weather conditions at the time.

A strong north or northwest wind would bring the acrid smell of locomotive coal smoke from the freight trains as they labored up the grade. When Mom would smell the coal smoke, she'd hurry us to help get her washing in off the clothesline before the sheets were salted and silted with coal soot. On Friday, a northwest wind would bring the smell of the cattle yards out at the end of Feeman Avenue where they were having auction sales.

To walk into Mom's garden in August was always a treat. Tomato vines, as you know, have their own characteristic smell. But to pick a nice, big Beefsteak, Ox-heart, or Burpees Big Boy, take it in the house, wash and slice it, and then sit down with a salt shaker and a piece of bread and butter was a treat fit for a King (or a Queen, to be politically correct).

Frequently, in the fall, I would walk into the house to the smell of apples stewing on the stove. Whenever we would have a heavy windstorm or rain in late summer, Mom would send me out to the back yard afterwards to pick up all the apples that had blown off the trees (the windfall). They would all be mixed together: Winesaps, Delicious, and Jonathans. I would take them all in to Mom. She would then wield her paring knife like a surgeon's scalpel and salvage all the edible portions from the bruises, wormholes and rotten areas. Then it would be dealer's choice: we'd either get apple dumplings, apple crisp, apple pie or stewed apples, depending on what her skillful eyes and hands determined was the best option.

In the wintertime, when my neighborhood pals and I would be making a snow fort, or an igloo, or whatever, Mom could tell by the pitch of our voices or an occasional unacceptable word that we all needed a time out. She'd call us into the basement and make us take off our wet, snowy clothes. Then we came up the stairs to the wonderful aroma of hot chocolate with a big, old "marshmaller," floating on the top. The smell and taste were all there!

Down in Baxter's woods in the fall, we were beckoned again by different smells and tastes. There were the woodsy smells of oaks, hickories, beeches, and walnut trees as we gathered more nuts for Mom's larder. While gathering nuts for Mom, I'd search for bunches of bittersweet to accent her decorations.

One special taste that I simply must mention again is that of Dr. Pepper. I know you remember my telling you about "discovering" it back in Chapter 5. I guess I always felt something special about Dr. Pepper because of first learning about it on a vacation far from Lima as a kid.

In Downtown Lima, there was the smell of Dome's Nut Shop with the hot, roasted redskins and that ever-pervading smell of caramel corn. And there was the smell of Hannah's Fish Market in the old High Street Market, too.

In late October, my parents and I always went to "the Ottawa Fair" (we never called it by its official name of the "Putnam County Fair"). It was always the last county fair of the season in our area. Because of the time of year, we were always blessed with either an Indian summer day or a cold frosty winter day. There were mingled smells of fresh horse manure from the harness horses and the gas fumes of the tractors on display. Occasionally, Dad would take me over around to the Speed Barns where they kept the racehorses. There I was introduced to the smell of alcohol from an open flask because as we walked past the stalls, we would occasionally come upon two or three guys who were "getting an early start on the day."

Also at the Fair, they had the best fish sandwiches, and Hoky-Poky ice cream in bars so hard you could drive a nail with one. There was also cotton candy, caramel apples and wonderful salt-water taffy to eat on the way home...

One last taste reference that sticks in my memory is the first soft ice cream I ever tasted. Probably thirty or forty years before Dairy Queen, this was sold down at Russell's Point Amusement Park and was called "Barr's Frozen Frostola." It was frozen custard, and I have yet to find any that approaches it.

As you go through life, keep sniffing and tasting . . . and sooner or later, like a moment on Candid Camera, "when you least expect it," you, too will be transported back to one of those golden smells or tastes from your childhood.

Leaving Home

*This wasn't really what
I'd had in mind . . .*

29. The Murrays of Hazel Avenue Take on WWII

In 1938, Adolph Hitler exacted his demands from the British and French. Neville Chamberlain called them "negotiations for peace" but in reality, it was appeasement of the Third Reich. The British conducted a national poll at the time and ten million out of the eleven million total Brits voted, "No war with Germany under any circumstances!"

A lone member of Parliament, who was frequently booed, managed to get legislation passed to update the Royal Air Force and to increase their depleted Armed Forces. That was Winston Churchill. After Hitler took the Sudeten lands, and then Poland, France was next. Their Maginot Line was absolutely no hindrance to the *Wehrmacht*.

When the Stuka and Fokker bombers eventually began bombing London, the Brits realized the folly of their ways. Winston Churchill continued almost single-handedly to put the backbone back into England. Then he began courting FDR and the U.S. He was able to talk Roosevelt into the "Lend/Lease Program" to supply Britain with the Materiel of War: tanks, planes, ships and ammunition.

The Americans polled voted 67% for keeping out of Europe's problems, as they remembered World War One. Senator Bob Taft of Ohio was one of the leading isolationists, along with Senator Vandenberg of Michigan. However, on September 16, 1940 the first-ever peacetime Selective Service Bill was passed. All men between the ages of 18 and 36 were required to register with the draft. After all the registrants had signed up, General Hershey began the "lottery", picking the "winners", the first ones to be drafted. They were all sent the same letter that began "Greetings." Then instructions followed to report at a certain date and time to some central place in their town, to be transported from there to an Induction Center.

They were instructed to "just bring enough clothes for three days" because, if you passed the exam, you would not be returning home anyway and the Government would be supplying all your clothes for your tour of duty. (This military clothing is called "G.I.", short for "government issue".) A song of those days had the lines "Just bring enough clothes for three days cause they ain't gonna turn you loose." The proposed tour of duty was to be for one year; hence another popular song of the day that went "Goodbye, Dear, I'll be back in a year."

Well, the Murray Involvement began in September of 1941 when my brother, Kenneth, got his selective service summons. He went for basic training at Camp Stewart in Georgia. After basic, he was sent to Camp Davis, NC, for training in an anti-aircraft battalion. The "ack-ack" guns he was trained to use (40mm Bofor anti-aircraft guns) were to keep the German dive-bombers off our troops.

Following Ken's ack-ack training, he went to Ft. Eustis , VA, and was assigned to a regiment of the First Army. After December 7 (Pearl Harbor) he wrote home and said "Don't look for me home in a year!"

In 1942, Ken did come home, but only on a furlough. Unfortunately, my older brother, Marvin, was away at Indiana University, pursuing a degree in organic chemistry at the time and didn't get to see him.

While he was home, Ken and I talked more in one week than we had in my previous 16 years. He told me that I should start preparing myself because I would be in the service as soon as I graduated from high school. I told him, "You older guys will have them whipped before I graduate!" and he said "No, this is going to be a long war!" The next thing I knew, Ken was in England, providing anti-aircraft coverage for the American installations there. He was to serve an extended tour in England while waiting for D-Day.

Meanwhile, my brother, Marvin, who was ten years older than me, received his notice at college to report to Camp Atterbury, Indiana, for induction. From there, he went to Jefferson Barracks in St. Louis for basic training. He was supposed to go into a chemical warfare unit because of his organic chemistry knowledge. However, he was sent to Lowry Field in Denver, Colorado and because of his knowledge of mathematics, physics and optics, he became a "Norden Bomb Sight" specialist and was assigned to the 13th Air Force.

The next year Marvin came home on furlough just as I was graduating from high school in June, 1943. He asked me what my plans were and I said, "I guess I'll get a job until I'm drafted." He very forcefully said, *"No, you're not!* You were in a college prep course and you are not *fit* to do any work! Believe me, you must get all the education you can

169

before you have to go into the Army or *you will end up in the Infantry, which is a death sentence!*"

He acquired the entrance forms from Ohio State and told me to sit down and fill them out. I replied that I didn't know what courses or college to enter, and he said, "You'd better think of something quick because I'm going to mail those forms before I leave here!"

So, on the spur of the moment, I chose a pre-veterinary course. Marvin took the forms and mailed them, and about ten days after I graduated from high school, I found myself as a summer freshman at Ohio State University, and scared to death.

Marvin went back to Lowry, and his unit was soon mobilized, and he went off to the South Pacific.

After I got over the shock of being in college, I went over to the Arts College to talk to the dean, who was a counselor. We discussed my dilemma of wanting to get into vet school while still facing selective service when I became eighteen. He recommended that I enlist in the Enlisted Reserve Corps (ERC) before I did become eighteen and have to register for the draft. "Then," he said, "you'll get accepted into vet school and the Army won't call you up because they need vets here. But you have to do all this before you become eighteen!"

So I went home and got my parents' permission to enlist. They didn't take to it too well, but they signed the papers.

Then I went back to Columbus and to the recruiting office, and enlisted on August 17, the day just before I became eighteen. I raised my hand, said "I do" and became a member of the ERC, and indeed I didn't have to register for the draft.

My next step was to get into vet school, so I went over to the school and talked to a Dean Brumley. He said my grades were very satisfactory and then he asked, "Do you have any military commitments?" I proudly said, "Yes, I'm in the Enlisted Reserve Corps." He frowned and said, "I can't touch you."

Stunned, I exclaimed, "But Dean Guthrie told me that that is what I had to do!" Brumley said "I'm sorry, but Dean Guthrie doesn't know what he is talking about."

So, there I was, enlisted in the Army with no way I could "un-enlist." What a revolting development!

Well, early the next year I was indeed ordered to report to Ft. Thomas, Kentucky on Feb. 14, 1944. I was there for a month on KP while they decided what to do with me. I was glad to peel potatoes, though, because all the troop shipments from Ft. Thomas were going to Camp Blanding, Florida, to the infantry.

Finally they decided to send me to the medics at Camp Barkley, Texas, just outside of Abilene. I went through basic training there and have lots of material from boot camp for another story. After all the marches, infiltration courses, immunizations, etc., I was put on a train and sent to Lawson General Hospital outside of Atlanta for training to become an X-ray technician.

In X-ray School

After four months, I got a ten-day furlough home. While there, I saw Mom's three-star flag or banner hanging in the front window, signaling that she had three boys in the service. I then went back to Camp Barkley for assignment into a General Hospital for the Army, which was to be somewhere in Europe.

And I was indeed given instructions to join the 241st General Hospital, and immediately began my journey to it. We got on a train and went to Camp Kilmer, New Jersey, where we got training with gas masks, and awaited assignment to a ship that would take us to Europe. We were assigned to the ship Isle de France, and on a cold, wet, snowy day in November, 1944 we boarded what would be our home for the next nine days until she docked in Greenock, Scotland.

From Scotland we went to a small town south of Manchester, called Knutsford, and lived in Quonset huts till we embarked for France on New Years Eve 1944.

If I may explain: a "Quonset hut" was like a cylinder split down the middle and laid on its side, with the curved dome at the top and the linear side edges on the ground. The two ends would be sealed with lumber, and each had a door. The sizes varied, and a soldier would put the foot of his cot up against the curving side wall so you could house many soldiers in one hut. The huts were also used as bath facilities and latrines and in England the signs above read "ABLUTIONS," which I always felt was somehow amusing. There were entire army camps composed of various-sized Quonset Huts

To cap off our family's involvement: while all of this overseas action was going on with the three Murray sons, the Murray daughter, Mary, had graduated from the Ohio State School for the Deaf and became employed as an inspector at the Timken Roller Bearing Plant, part of the defense industry.

So our parents had four children all in the war effort: three boys in the military service and a daughter in a defense plant.

More escapades were to follow . . . and they will be presented in the next story.

173

Look Out, Adolf and Tojo . . .

30.   "Here Come the Murrays!"

When we left our saga a short page ago, it was February of 1944. Ken was someplace in England awaiting the invasion of France, Marvin was somewhere in the South Pacific with the 13th Air Force, and I was going through my training and assignment to a General Hospital, headed for England and then to France.

On June 6, 1944, the momentous D-Day (Invasion of Normandy) occurred. Everything was thereafter dated "D-Day plus (whatever day it was after June 6th)."

On D-Day plus 6, Kenneth waded ashore with his equipment at Cherbourg, France with his unit. Their function was to supply anti-aircraft fire to keep the German *Luftwaffe* from bombing and strafing the Yanks along with their supplies and ammunition. The Americans were in intense battles throughout Normandy, and Ken's was the first Combat Team to cross the vaunted "Siegfried Line." They captured the German town of Aachen.

Ken's luck ran out here. He and his Lieutenant and three others were up front scouting a new position for their ack-ack guns. Unfortunately, they had gotten in front of their own infantry lines and drew fire from a German "Tiger-88" cannon, which was more powerful and more accurate than our 105 Howitzers. As the shells exploded around them, the Lieutenant, who had stepped on a land mine, and the other three men, were killed, and Ken, the only one surviving, had numerous shrapnel wounds. At least one slug went into his chest and collapsed a lung. Fortunately an Infantry medic got to him quickly, applied a bandage, gave him a shot of morphine, and brought help to get him to a field hospital. From there he was evacuated out of France to a U.S. Army hospital south of Manchester.

My dad was working at a construction site for Green and Sawyer when he was tracked down by a Western Union delivery man. The messenger handed Dad a telegram from the President of the U.S. that said "I regret to inform you that First Sgt. Kenneth A. Murray has been wounded in action and has been evacuated to England."

Of course, that was a bombshell for Mom and Dad.

Meanwhile, my unit, the 241st General Hospital, had embarked on the ship Isle de France, and, eluding the German Wolfpacks of submarines, landed in Scotland. When we subsequently arrived in Knutsford to await shipment to France, the nurses in our hospital there were placed on "detached service" at a U.S. Army hospital 25 miles away.

It just so happened that this was the very hospital where Ken was recuperating! Ken overheard one of the nurses say that she was from the 241st General, and he knew that was my outfit. He tried to get word to me through the Red Cross that he had been wounded and was only twenty-five miles away! However, I didn't get the information until I had left England and been in France for several weeks.

Now, our arrival in France, which was my first entry during the war onto soil recently held by the Germans, went as follows: We walked off our channel crossing ship onto a metal dock at Le Havre on New Year's Eve 1944. Traveling on a troop train during the night, we woke up the next morning in the bombed out coastal town of Etretat (which happens to be the birthplace of Victor Hugo).

The Battle of the Bulge was in progress and our hospital was slotted to go into the Belgian area of the bulge. The 82nd Airborne was up in the Ardennes fighting, so we were sent to a little village called Sisson, France, to the base camp of the 82nd Airborne.

We set up our hospital and began taking the wounded from the 82nd and other units on the front, which was just 30 miles away. Because of the terrible cold, many of our patients had frozen feet, toes and fingers. The men of the 82nd really loved their General, who would visit their front unannounced. One soldier told me that once in his foxhole some one tapped him on the shoulder and said, "How're you doin' soldier?" He looked around and saw that it was General Gavin.

The tide of the war turned, and the Yanks and the British accepted the surrender of the Germans on May 6, 1945, less than a year after the Invasion! (The Italians had given up long before.)

Well, the world had been shocked three weeks before on April 13, 1945 when President Franklin D. Roosevelt died and Vice President Harry S.Truman was sworn in as President. Most of the men in our

176

outfit were depressed at the loss of FDR, but President Truman took over and made all the right decisions.

About four months later, on Monday, August 6, 1945, the Atomic Bomb was dropped on Hiroshima and, several days later, another A-bomb was dropped on Nagasaki. That did it for the Japs, and the Japanese statesmen like Prime Minister Tojo groomed the somewhat out-of-touch Emperor Hirohito for the surrender.

After V-E day in May, our unit had been sent to Camp Lucky Strike, a replacement depot, in preparation for shipping out to the China-Burma-India theater. But after the Japanese surrendered, our orders were changed (whew!), and we were sent to Paris to take over the 23rd General Hospital in the Hopital de La Pitie, a 2,000 bed hospital (no small facility) shared by the Army with the French.

While in Paris, I had an encounter with Marlene Dietrich at a subway stop along with my hospital buddies, but that will require a story all to itself.

I had accumulated enough "service points" to go home, but I was re-classified as "essential," as were all X-ray technicians. I was transferred to a "Graves Registration Service" and was sent to a two-week school to learn "how to identify unknown dead bodies."

Following this uplifting education, I was transferred to Fulda, Germany, and then to a Graves Registration unit in French-occupied Germany. That was the most gruesome job I had ever had, and when

177

my Lieutenant said he needed a clerk typist, I showed him on my MOS (military occupation services) report that I could type. And so my high school typing course miraculously rescued me from becoming an alcoholic!

I handled all the records for seven units in the field. I never worked harder nor enjoyed it more than when I was rescued from that "identification job"!

Meanwhile, Marvin, along with the 13th Air Force, had made it from base to base in the South Pacific. After MacArthur liberated the Philippines, Marvin was stationed in the Philippines and began work on his assignment of learning the native language of "Tagalog." While there, he developed infectious hepatitis, as did many of the airmen. He was treated and was eventually sent home back to the United States, and was mustered out from Camp Atterbury, where he had gone into the service.

I was the last of the Murrays to get into the service, and the last to be discharged. Our work in the French Occupation Zone was finally completed and I had more than enough points to go home. During my tour of duty I had advanced from Private to the rank of Technical Sergeant ("T- Sergeant").

Perhaps I should explain the ranking system, for those not familiar.

There are two kinds of soldiers: enlisted (including non-commissioned officers) and commissioned officers who could receive their commission in four ways:
1. West Point Academy
2. Officers Training School

3. Reserve Officers Training School (ROTC)
4. Battle Field "Direct" Commission
(Had Ken not been wounded, he may have received a Battle Field commission when his commanding officer was killed.) All the candidates who received these commissions were commissioned as "An Officer and a Gentleman" of the Army.

There is a caste system in the Army. The enlisted men and non-commissioned officers are not allowed to mingle socially with the commissioned officers. They each even have their own mess halls, tap rooms and stores. The Army believes that "familiarity breeds contempt," which means that fraternization causes a breakdown in discipline that could be dangerous in time of battle. It is the same way in the Navy, Air Force and the Marines. This is a simplified list of basic rank order:

1	Private
2	Private First-Class
3	Corporal
4	Sergeant ("Buck Sergeant")
5	Staff Sergeant
6	First Sergeant
7	Master Sergeant
8	Warrant Officer
9	Lieutenant
10	Captain
11	Major
12	Colonel
13	Brigadier General
14	Major General
15	Lieutenant General
16	General of the Army

Added to this list were T-ratings denoting technical skills: in my case, X-ray technology. I had advanced from Private to T-Corporal and then on to Tech Sergeant. The T-Corporals and T-Sergeant ranks were given for recognition and for awarding comparable pay scales. As far as authority was concerned, the T-Sergeants were outranked by the straight non-commissioned officers except within their technical specialties.

The second-highest enlisted rating was Master Sergeant topped by First Sergeant, usually the head of a company of soldiers (four platoons of eight men each). Ken was a First Sergeant.

Anyway, back to our story: the Lieutenant tried to talk me into re-enlisting by dangling duty in Norway, Sweden, and Denmark in front of me, but I told him, "I've really had a bellyful and I want to go home!"

I was sent to Hamburg to board the U.S. Pitston Victory ship headed for New York. While there, I learned that my outfit's orders had been changed from Norway, Sweden, and Denmark to Austria. I had been no fool.

As we sailed down the English Channel, I looked over and saw the "White Cliffs of Dover." It was a boisterous trip home and I finally had my first taste of Wonder Bread and fresh milk in over three years. We got our final pay on board ship and the dice games and poker games were rampant. I got into a poker game, lost 85 cents, and I've never played poker since then.

After disembarking in New York, I turned in all my equipment, blankets, overcoat, backpack etc. I just "kept enough clothes for 3 days" as I returned to Camp Atterbury, where Marvin had also been mustered out, to be turned loose on May 16, 1946.

I called home and told the folks I would be in on the 2:00 PM B&O train from Cincinnati. When I got into Lima, I jumped off the train with my duffle bag and there was Mom, Dad, First Sergeant Ken, and Corporal Marvin. I got vigorous hugs from them all.

When things calmed down, I hit my brother Marvin on the shoulder and said, "Corporal, would you put those bags in the trunk?" *Wham!* - I got hit upside the head and was told in no uncertain terms, "There will be no rank pulled around here, *T-Sergeant!*"

Well, Mary came home for next Sunday's dinner, and all the Murrays were finally back from the war, and Adolph and Tojo were no more. They had learned not to mess with The Murrays!

And Mom could now take down her three-star flag from the front window.

31. Doubling Back: My Introduction to the Army

(or, *How I Handled My First Crisis*)

My introduction to the Army was not supposed to happen! Two separate situations arose that looked like they would get me deferred. But, as you will see, they were but fool's gold and Uncle Sam got his way.

Some of this story was related just previously, so if some of it is a rehash for you, please just skip ahead!

The year was 1943. I was 17 years old and a freshman at Ohio State University, right out of high school. I had chosen a pre-veterinarian curriculum and was interested in getting into vet school. However, the Army looked like it might intervene if I didn't take measures.

So I went over to the Arts College and talked to the Dean. He told me about a program in the army called the Enlisted Reserve Corps. The plan he laid out was that, first, the army definitely wouldn't call me to active duty until six months after I enlisted in this special group. This would give me time to apply to vet school and, if my grades were good, I'd get accepted. Then the army wouldn't take me after all because they needed veterinarians badly, and they would let me finish school.

The only catch was that I had to enlist into this program while I was still 17 or I wouldn't be eligible for it. I was soon to have my 18th birthday, so I went and got the application, which required that I have my parents sign their permission.

I hitchhiked home and presented the plan to Mom and Dad. This was 1943, and their two oldest sons were already in the army, and Mom wasn't about to let her baby sign up. I reasoned and jawboned and told them that if I got accepted to vet school, the army wouldn't want to take me out of school. I finally sold Mom, and she and Dad signed the application for enlistment.

I hurried back to Columbus, went out to the recruiting office and, the day before I was 18 (August 17), I raised my hand, said "I do" and became Private Murray -- with the promise that they wouldn't call me to active duty for six months.

The next week, I went over to the vet school and had an appointment with the Admissions Officer, Dean Brumley, and I told him that I would like to be admitted to the College of Veterinary Medicine. He looked at my grades and told me that they were satisfactory.

Then he asked, "Do you have any Military commitments?" and at that point, I proudly told him that I was in the Enlisted Reserve Corps. He got a frown on his face and said sadly, "Sorry, I can't touch you."

I said, "But the Dean in the Arts School said that enlisting was what I should do!" He said, "Unfortunately, the Dean didn't know what he was talking about!"

Well, the fat was in the fire! There was no way I could un-enlist and so I dreadfully awaited the six-month call-up date. Right on schedule, I got my notice to appear at Ft. Thomas, Kentucky on February 14, 1944 for induction.

Now it so happens that, about a month before then, I had developed a middle ear infection and went over to the student health center. The doctor there told me that he wanted to see me in a week to see if the medicine had done its job. I said, "Sorry, Doctor, but I'll be in the Army by then." He said, "Oh, no, you won't! You have a large perforation in your eardrum and they won't take you. I know that because I do the army physicals here at Ft. Hayes."

Well, it looked like I had a second escape route and, with that bit of good news, I went home and decided not to tell Mom and Dad about my ear, so that it would be a surprise when, about a week from then, I'd appear back home with a deferment! I remember the morning they took me to the B&O train station to go to Cincinnati en route to Kentucky. It was dark. I had a smirking smile as I kissed them good-bye. And they were both crying.

Little did I realize that they had it right!

When I got to Cincinnati, I took a streetcar over to Ft. Thomas, Kentucky and presented myself to the induction officer, as did several hundred others. I spent the morning going through clothing lines for shoes, socks, underwear, wool shirts and pants, a coat, fatigue pants, a shirt, and a duffle bag -- all the things I would need to look like a soldier.

184

I went to the company office and was assigned to a billet (bunkhouse) by the 1st Sergeant who was a burly guy and appeared to be the type not to have a ready ear. It was late afternoon when I went to my billet, and I claimed a lower bunk.

While I was putting my blankets on the bed and my clothes in the duffel bag, I noticed that a button on my shirt collar was just about to fall off. So I go out my pocket sewing kit and began to sew the button back on.

(Here I have to depart from my story a bit. When I had become a serious hunter earlier in life, one of my brothers had given me a field-dressing knife for Christmas. It fit nicely in my hand, had a beautiful red-and-white-striped handle, a razor-sharp blade of about four inches in length, and a spring release button that made it, technically, a switchblade. The spring release made it handy to open while wearing gloves. I had naturally brought it with me to the Army, as I had carried it in my pocket ever since I had owned it.)

As I sat there sewing, a loud, raucous voice rang out from an ugly redneck about 5 ft. 4 inches tall, weighing 250 pounds, with a three-day growth of beard and a mouth full of rotten teeth. He said, "Well, now! I've found an Army sweetheart!"

I knew that the prisons were discharging inmates early and the draft boards were sending them on to the Army. It didn't take me long to realize the situation I was faced with. I knew that the 1st Sergeant would be of no help, so I figured that this would be my baptism of fire.

The speaker, Bubba, came over to where I sat and put a hand on my shoulder. I knocked it off and stood up, but he started backing me into a corner. My right hand shot down into my pants pocket and out came my rabbit-gutting knife. I pushed the button and, with a loud click, the nasty-looking knife blade sprang out.

Bubba's eyes became like saucers as he looked at the knife and I said, loud enough for just him to hear, "If you ever lay a hand on me again, or ever touch me, be ready to spend the rest of the day picking your guts up off the floor."

Bubba backed off and never came near me again.

Nor did anyone else.

Well, it turned out that I never *did* get my medical deferment, even with the ear problem.

And I carried that knife through the entire time I was in the service and then later throughout pre-med and medical school. I don't know where or when I lost track of my life-saving knife, but it certainly served its purpose in many ways. Other than during that army incident, I never displayed the knife or threatened anyone else with it, and I doubt that there were more than four people who knew that I always carried a field knife, spring-loaded.

What did I learn that day?

1. We do not remember days, but we remember moments.

2. Faith is the ability not to panic (especially if you have your favorite knife in your hands).

32. My Entry into the Tall Tale Contest

This yarn goes back to the summer of 1947.

I had been mustered out of the Army, had re-entered the pre-medical curriculum at Ohio State University, and was in my third year of pre-med.

There was a program called the Arts / Med which (if you were lucky enough to get accepted) would allow you to enter medical school with only three years of pre-med. They would count the first year of medicine as the fourth year of your Bachelor of Arts Degree.

At that time, the monthly stipend for a single veteran on the GI Bill was $50 a month. I was paying $25 a month rent, so that didn't leave much for food, laundry and Friday night beer.

In the Army, I had been trained as an X-ray technician. I had heard that some of the medical students were getting room, board and laundry for taking X-rays at night. So, I took a bus out to Mt. Carmel Hospital and went up to the X-ray dept. to see the radiologist, a Dr. Fulton.

I inquired as to their need for a night technician who was experienced and he took me down to see the Sister Superior right away. We chatted and she allowed as how the present technicians were getting tired of night call and that they just might be able to find a place for me. I was to live in the intern's quarters and I would get room, board, and laundry for taking emergency X-rays every night and every other weekend. She drove a hard bargain, but I needed her offerings and so I moved into the intern's quarters.

They were all a nice group of medical students and bore me no resentment even though I was a lowly plebe. They would even give me a ride over to the University in the mornings. The interns' quarters were noisy in the evenings, so I would go up to the X-ray department to study, and if there was any business from the Emergency Room, I would be right there.

One summer evening, I was studying, and a bit bored, so I turned on the radio on the desk. A program called "The Tall Tale Contest" came on, and they said that whoever sent in the tallest tale for the week would win a free weekend at the Deshler Wallick Hotel. They read the winner for the previous week and I thought that I could do better than that, so I copied down the address and resolved to join their liars contest.

The next night, after I had finished my assignments, I wrote out a tale that I thought would win, and mailed it. Several weeks passed and I forgot all about my entry.

One day I went up to the X-ray department, ostensibly on business, but I really wanted to see a cute secretary who worked up there named Pauline List. She asked me if I had entered a contest at a radio station and said that the station had called to see if I worked there or if I were a patient there. She gave me a number to call the station and -- lo and behold! -- I had won the contest, and the letter and the hotel reservation would be in the mail for the next weekend!

So when the time came, I packed my small suitcase, and drove seven blocks east and checked in to the hotel. I called Pauline and she didn't believe that I was in the hotel, so I described the room in detail. I invited her up to see the room but she refused the invitation. She did, however, agree to have dinner with me in the hotel dining room and we had an evening of dancing afterward.

And so, that was my introduction to tall tale telling. The radio station said it was quite a good story and thanked me for participating. The tale I told goes as follows:

> When I was a youngster in high school, I had a pet fox squirrel. Now, this wasn't just an ordinary squirrel. He was the fastest tree-climbing squirrel in the world! Naturally, with such a valuable squirrel, I pampered him a lot, with a special padded cage that was heated in the winter.
>
> Each day when I would come home from school, I would exercise my squirrel and I would let him out of his cage. We had a tall walnut tree, about 100 feet tall, in the middle of our back yard. That squirrel would circle the back yard about three times to pick up speed, then --WHOOSH! -- up the tree he would go, knock off a walnut, race back down, and be there to catch it before it hit the ground!
>
> Well, one day I was late in getting home from school. We had had a severe thunder and lightening storm the night before, and a bolt of lightening had hit

190

that walnut tree slap dab at the bottom and knocked it down. Since I was late coming home, Mom thought the squirrel needed to be let out of his cage; she had completely forgotten about the walnut tree's being felled. And when that squirrel got out of his cage, he circled the back yard three times and climbed 100 feet in the air before he realized that tree wasn't there!

- - -

I wouldn't want to forget to tell you that the secretary, Pauline, and I later married, had a family, and have been happily together for over 53 years.

And *that* tale is a *true* one!

Pauline and I today

Odds and Ends

*Enjoying a last few moments of relief after
med school graduation in the shrine known
as Buckeye Stadium.*

33. The Singing in My Life

About a year ago, Polly and I went to a patriotic symphony performance in Naples at the Philharmonic. The children's chorus in the production so impressed me that I felt it necessary to revisit my grade school days and do a story on my six years spent there in elementary education ("Horace Mann Grade School, Revisited").

Well, it happened again! Last Saturday night, Polly and I attended the Southwest Florida Symphony "Pops" performance, featuring the Southwest Florida Symphony, the Southwest Florida Chorale and the Children's Chorus. They presented a program of Rodgers and Hammerstein, with excerpts of songs from *South Pacific, Carousel, The King and I, The Sound of Music* and *Oklahoma*.

I guess I'm a pushover for children's choruses and, when a talented soprano led them through "Doe, a Deer" from *The Sound of Music*, I found a tear in my eye and a lump in my throat. My thoughts returned to my own introduction to "Do, Re, Mi" by our grade school music instructor, and I decided to do this story on the singing in my life.

Mrs. Lewis, our second grade music teacher, had a gadget that held five pieces of chalk and, with one fell swoop, she could produce five parallel lines on the black board to form a musical staff. Then she took us through "do, re, mi, fa, sol, la, ti, do" -- not as elaborately as Julie Andrews did in *The Sound of Music*, taking her charges through "Doe, a female deer; Re, a drop of golden sun, Mi, a name I call myself," and so on. But still we did learn our scales, and through the next four years progressed to folk songs and ballads.

We mastered The Sailor's Hornpipe, Billy Boy ("Can she bake a cherry pie?"), The Hole In The Window, Go Tell Aunt Rhodie ("the old grey goose is dead"), The Fox is On the Town-O, and many others.

While in grade school and junior high, I was recruited (by a shove from my mom) into the Calvary E & R Youth Choir. It was led by a professional music teacher who taught singing privately for a living, but who took us kids on gratis as a tribute to God.

She was of German heritage and was a large, stern woman who reminded me of a Brunhilde from a Wagnerian Opera. She tolerated no nonsense and she cajoled, threatened and successfully extracted some beautiful Handelian music from a bunch of indifferent kids.

I was a boy soprano then, and when she asked me if I would like to sing some solos of "He Leadeth Me" and "I Know That My Redeemer Liveth," I was too scared to say no. I knew my mom would have been disappointed had I not agreed.

As is always true, we don't realize that we have a great teacher until years later, and we certainly had one in her. We even traveled to other churches to put on concerts. When my voice began to change, I wasn't exactly a Nelson Eddy, Perry Como, or a Bing Crosby. I sounded more like Don Knotts, so I didn't sing in any choral groups in high school.

My next participatory singing was when I was eighteen and in basic training in the Army. On our 25-mile marches we would sing in time with the marching. We would sing "I've got sixpence, jolly, jolly sixpence" and "I had a good home, but I left, right, left, right" and the Army's caisson song ("Over hill, over dale"), and "Rolling Home." This helped the time pass till we got back to camp and could soak and treat the blisters on our feet.

When we shipped from Camp Kilmer to Scotland and then down to Knutsford, south of Manchester, we were billeted near a medieval-style church that was built in the early 1500's. Our outfit, the 241st General Hospital, organized a choir to help kill time while awaiting a boat to France. It was there that I learned the harmony for Praetorius' "Lo, How A Rose E'er Blooming."

After the shooting war was over, our hospital was transferred to Paris, and there my music education progressed. I saw and heard three beautiful operas in the Paris Opera House. I saw *Aida* and *Rigoletto,* which were spectacular, and Beethoven's only opera, *Fidelio.*

Music, for me, stopped during my studying for pre-med. Once I got into medical school, the four of us assigned to our cadaver would sometimes break into four-part barbershop harmony to relieve the tension and stress. I sang the lead, Bill Grannis, the alto, Jack Cox, the tenor, and Dale South, the bass. At the end of the three-hour dissecting lab, we would harmonize on "Dry Bones" and "Git on Board, Little Chillun'"! The other guys in the lab would gather round to listen till one day, Dr. Graves, the professor of anatomy, walked in with raised eyebrows, and everyone dispersed like a covey of quail being flushed by a bird dog. That pretty much put a damper on our singing in anatomy.

After graduation and during our internship, three of us, Grannis, Cox and Murray were still together. Ed Burns joined us and, once again, we would raise the lovely tones of "Lo How a Rose E'er Blooming." We would sing late at night down in the Emergency Room, which wasn't busy then the way they are today. We weren't too shabby and we were even asked to sing for the Nurses' Christmas Party.

In the mid-1950's, my practice was thriving, and Polly and I joined the Cotillion Club, which was a formal dance club complete with formal attire, dance cards, and three or four dinner dances each year. At the end of these dances, when the orchestra was packing up to leave, Dick Dodson, Cece Baylor, Jack Stuber and I would lock step into four-part harmony with such songs as:
"Wait 'Til the Sun Shines, Nelly,"
"Tell Me Why,"
"When You Wore a Tulip,"
"I Was Seeing Nelly home," and
"By the Light of the Silvery Moon."
The band had had their chance and were leaving and now it was our turn. Soon our wives would single us out with "It's time to go!", "We have to get the baby sitter home!", and so forth

I was a busy family doctor but never too busy to go hear our children in Lima Senior's "Holiday in Harmony," "The Messiah Sing," or the season-ending productions of musicals. They were a great part of our music education.

So that's my span and my story -- from Do Re Mi, to folk tunes, to Messiah excerpts, to marching songs in the Army, to operas in Paris, and on to barbershop singing in anatomy lab and at the Cotillion Club. I've got a taste for folk singing, ballads, barbershopping, Broadway musicals, some operas, and music by Bach, Brahms, Beethoven, Mendelssohn, Handel, Mozart and Smetana.

But, please -- no Bartok!

Singing has been great fun, but since no one has ever offered me a contract, I don't think I'll quit my day job!

34. The First Doctor in Allen County, Ohio

(Written for my Memoirs Class and based on a speech I used to give at the Allen County Museum)

My name is Emmett Murray and this is my wife, Polly. Before I retired in 1995, I had been a Family Physician for 42 years.

Polly was a master homemaker who raised four great children. While I was busy with my practice, she was active in the PTA, was a room mother for many years, and ran the school carnivals and bake sales. In addition, she spent many years in the Medical Auxiliary as legislative and membership chairman. She also spent 10 years as a Red Cross Volunteer, and was a docent at our Allen County Historical museum when I retired, which leads me to my story.

After I retired, I had some free time, so I went down to the Museum to see what was going on. Shortly thereafter, I took the Docent training course and became a docent. As it turned out, they had a medical display that needed updating.

I became interested in who the first Doctor in Allen County was. To get an understanding of things, I had to do some research. This is what I found:

The Northwest Territory was acquired from the French in 1783 and was referred to as "the Ohio Country." It was all the land above the Ohio River west of Pennsylvania and east of the Mississippi.

To apply for statehood, a territory had to have 60,000 voting males (women's suffrage hadn't occurred as yet). Ohio became a state in 1803 (then, in order: Indiana, in 1812; Illinois, in 1818; Michigan in 1837; and Wisconsin in1848). The Northwest Territorial Ordinance forbade slavery, guaranteed trial by jury, provided freedom of religion and worship, and declared that free public education would be forever encouraged.

In the early years of our country, there were two ways of becoming a doctor. First, there were medical schools in Boston, Baltimore, New York and Philadelphia. A student would go and listen to lectures for two years and, if he could pass the examinations, he would be given the diploma of Doctor of Medicine.

The second way was for a student to "read medicine" for seven years with a practicing doctor. The student would have to pay the doctor a fee of $100 (a fortune in those days) and agree to assist the doctor in all ways. These involved caring for the doctor's horses, harness, saddle and buggy; tending the herb and medicinal garden; sweeping out the office; keeping all the records; and assisting the doctor's wife if she had any tasks for him. If they had a spare bedroom, he was allowed to sleep in the house; if not, he had to sleep in the barn.

For all this, he was allowed to go on house calls with the doctor, assist the doctor as his proficiency increased, read the doctor's books on medicine and study the skeleton that was kept in the closet. If he performed well, he was given a certificate, which allowed him to practice medicine after his seven years of apprentice ship.

In the Indian tribes, their medicine man was called a shaman (you may remember one of them whom I met in Chapter 4), and it is of interest to note that for a brave to become a shaman, he also had to serve a seven-year apprenticeship with the tribe's medicine man.

The Shawnee Indians lived along the banks of the Auglaize River in Allen County at the turn of the 19th century. They were a peaceful tribe and their medicine man, or shaman, would take care of the early settlers and their families.

In 1812, President James Madison sent a large number of troops into the Ohio Territory and he ordered Colonel Thomas Poague to clear and maintain a wagon path between St. Mary's and Fort Defiance. To protect his men and supplies, Poague built a fort on the banks of the Auglaize and named it Fort Amanda, after his wife.

The garrison contained a small hospital, and a doctor, Samuel Jacob Lewis, was assigned to Ft. Aman- da. Since he didn't have that much work to do in the fort, he offered to take care of the medical needs of the settlers, and soon became the first physician of Allen County.

Now this is not all there is to the story. Noel, my storytelling teacher, has told me that many stories contain a "comma," an important story within a story. And here is such a story:

Let us turn back the calendar to see where Dr. Jacob Lewis really came from ...

Our Allen County physician pioneer, Dr. Lewis, had had a life filled with hardships. He was one of seven children of a farm couple in New Jersey. When the British declared war on the Colonists, Jacob's father enlisted in General Washington's army, only to fall ill and die soon after his arrival in camp. Jacob's mother held the family together and kept the farm profitable.

But Jacob had always wanted to study medicine, so, soon after he finished his schooling, he arranged to become the apprentice to a physician in Somerset County, New Jersey.

Shortly before he had finished his first of seven years, he got word that some renegade Indians had abducted his sister from her home in Virginia! Jacob got permission from the doctor and left to search for his sister.

He traced her to the Miami River region of Ohio, and there he took a job with a construction company. One day, while working to help build a road, he happened to hear the cry "Heaven help me!" coming from a throng of Indian women that was passing by. He recognized that voice as his sister's!

With the help of some of his friends, he was able to rescue her, and then to elude an infuriated Indian search party that trailed them for several days! They made their way to Ft. Defiance, and from there to Ft Detroit. After recuperating for a while, he worked to earn money and buy a horse. He then put his sister on

203

the horse and led her over the frozen Northeast to their mother's home in New Jersey.

After a short while, he returned to his study with the doctor, finished his prescribed time and duties, married, and took his new bride to Hamilton, Ohio.

In 1813, he was appointed Surgeon of the First Regiment of the Ohio Militia and was sent to Fort Amanda, which, of course, is in Allen County. That's how we got him.

- - -

"And now you know the rest of the Story."

35.   Some Memories That Fell Through the Cracks

On my first tour through my memoirs, a few things fell through the cracks and I hope to gather them up now. I also would like to reinforce and stress certain of my recollections, and perhaps put them together better for you, to convey a more total impression.

- - -

My trips through Baxter's Woods with my school chum, Eldon, were some of my happiest memories. We would frequently hear squirrels chattering and scolding us as we walked. If it was near dark, we might hear a hoot owl, which always made us walk a little faster.

Occasionally, we would get a whiff of skunk that had gotten stirred up, and we tried to keep our distance from the source of that smell. Eldon pointed out to me that there were lots of hickory, oak, walnut, cottonwood, and sycamore trees, but that we only knew of two beechnut trees in the whole woods.

In the spring, the floor of the woods was alive with the smell of Sweet Williams, Jack in the Pulpit, and May Apple blossoms. If we had walnuts to hull, there was an acidic smell. (If we got any of the walnut juice on our hands, it took weeks to wear off.)

But I always slept well after a trip to Baxter's Woods.

- - -

At home, on Hazel Avenue, there were also many sounds, smells, and tastes. Mom had a bed of Lilies of the Valley along the north side of the house in the shade, and they smelled *so* good in the spring. It seemed like there were a few of these tiny flowers all summer long. Mom also always had a Rose of Sharon by the side door that smelled so *sweet*!

In the back, she had a sour cherry and a peach tree. The peach tree was her source of supply for small switches for whipping my bare legs if she caught me out in the street!

She also had a keyhole-shaped lily pond in the back, and it was my job in the winter to chop holes in the ice on it to prevent cracks in the cement. One winter, it was about ten degrees above zero, and I had just chopped a two-foot-wide hole in the deep end and was ready to chop a hole in the other end. I stepped backward and instantly landed in freezing water up to my waist! *WOW!* What a surprise!

- - -

Across the street was the ten acres that contained the Horace Mann School, the track and football practice fields, and the wooden bleachers of the old College Grounds. In the summer, the American Legion Drum and Bugle Corps. would practice their playing, marching and formations there under the lights. It was a treat to hear their stirring marching music. In the fall, at the football games, the hot dog concession had its own great aroma.

Another taste and smell that I frequently recall is that of Fleer's Double Bubble chewing gum. The other gun varieties of Blackjack, Pepsin, and Teaberry also had very pleasant tastes and aromas.

On our way walking home from a movie, we would always pass the Plezol Bakery, and the smell of baking bread would just drive us wild till we could get home and fix our own slices of bread and butter. Sometimes the butter would turn out to be margarine that hadn't been colored yellow yet and, though it looked like lard, it tasted like butter.

- - -

When I worked at the Lima Ice and Coal Company in the summer, my hours were from 3 PM til midnight. One of my jobs, you may recall, was to pull 300-pound ice blocks from the freezing brine tanks and to run them through the scoring machine after removing each block from its freezing canister. To do this, one had to work on top of the freezing tanks, on wooden palettes. Occasionally we would get a really strong whiff of ammonia which would send us out to the fresh air to wipe the tears from our eyes.

The Ice and Coal Company was adjacent to the Pennsylvania Railroad tracks, and we could always hear the blaring horn of the Broadway Limited when it was about a mile and a half away coming east towards us. The station was just three blocks further east of the ice house, so when the train stopped to pick up or let off passengers, the sleeping cars, and sometimes the dining and club cars, would be stopped right next to the ice plant. A few minutes and a couple of toots later, away the train would roll . . .

I never got home till about 1 AM, so Mom would let me sleep a little later than usual the next day till I would hear the clop-clop-clop of the horses' hooves on the bricks as they pulled the milk and ice wagons along our streets. Then there would commence, somewhere in the neighborhood, the whistling metallic sound of each shovelful of coal as it was thrown down the coal chute into a bin in someone's basement. By then, it would be time to get up anyway, to mow the grass before I had to go to work again at 3 PM.

On Sundays, our noon meal would often be interrupted by the sound of a certain airplane's buzzing the neighborhood. Everyone would put down their knives and forks and run out the front door to look up at the bi-plane circling overhead, wagging its wings, then flying off. The pilot had a sister who lived about two blocks from us.

- - -

One of my favorite places to go was to Uncle Charlie's and Aunt Lu's farm. When I would come home after a week's visit there, I would chide my mom (Aunt Lu's younger sister) about what great breakfasts Aunt Lu would whip up for us. While Uncle Charlie was out milking the cows and slopping the hogs and harnessing his mules Aunt Lu would be frying round steak, baking biscuits, frying potatoes (or maybe some mush), and making toast and coffee -- just a typically huge farm breakfast. Uncle Charlie would come in, go to the cleanup room, wash his face and hands, comb his hair and come out with a big smile, ready for the big breakfast.

Mom didn't like me to kid her too much about those breakfasts. Besides, Dad and my two older brothers had generally eaten the bacon and eggs, toast and oatmeal, and finished off the coffee from Mom's kitchen long before I got up, and they were gone, not leaving much behind to show for all Mom's trouble.

There were a lot of characteristic smells up there on the farm. The barrel that Uncle Charlie kept his liquid hog feed in had a sour winery smell and also smelled like buckwheat. The feed was made with whey and other ingredients that Uncle Charlie added. I liked to get out a big dipperful and slop the hogs. There was also a distinct smell to the horse collars and harnesses: kind of a leathery, salty smell mixed with horse liniment and arnica. It was great to go up there and feel like part of the action.

- - -

Back again at home, there was a particular smell of glue when you would put a patch on an inner tube for a car or bicycle. Mom would always point out to me to the smells she noted when she shopped. Once or twice a week we would go to Shafer's Meat Market where they had sawdust on the floor (a nice smell). Once I laughed when I heard her ask the counter man, "How much are your brains today?" Mom didn't appreciate my snickering.

She would also go to Schell's Book and Writing Supplies Store which had a distinctive musty aroma. Next door to Schell's was Horne's Pharmacy, which sold only medicines, and had an antiseptic and medicinal smell. On the other side of Schell's was the

Kewpee Hamburger Shop which had the best smell of all!

- - -

On Saturdays, Mr. Flory, a youngish Mennonite farmer with a red beard and characteristic straw hat, would come to our house impeccably dressed, with tie and shirt plus suspenders and trousers. He brought his wares of strawberries, eggs, and chickens. He was always a very mild- and pleasant-natured man, and he would deliver chickens live or dressed.

- - -

I guess that takes care of most of what has fallen through the cracks. But let me assure you, nothing in the past seventy years of *MY* life has dimmed the taste of Fels naptha soap, applied in the mouth to clean up the language, or the stinging of a peach switch on bare legs!

Afterwords

My wife Polly, sister Mary, brother Marvin's wife Sudie, and my mom, Faye – all generally having the last and best word . . .

36. Storytelling in Dad's Life
(*By Robb Murray*)

Now that you have enjoyed some of Dad's stories in written form, I would like to venture a few observations for you about how these stories relate to Dad's lifelong enjoyment of all stories. I am Dad and Mom's second-born son and write from that perspective.

If you know Dad personally, you know how much he likes to tell funny stories. When he said in his Foreword that he believes laughter is essential to good health, we in his family know how much he has exemplified this belief throughout his life.

In addition to retelling football and fishing stories to his patients, just joking with them was a real treat for Dad. He repeated many a hilarious tale to them during office visits, which they would always make a point of telling the rest of our family when we ran into them around Lima. Each time over the years that the kids in our family have come back to visit our parents, Dad has always had five or six new stories to roll out during mealtimes. He is egged on by Mom, on whom he practices his material, and who always seems to find his jokes just as funny the twentieth time as the first.

I can't speak in detail about exactly how humor helped Dad in his practice, but clearly it benefited all involved. Dad always displays a genuine affection for both his material and his listeners, both patients and civilians. His jokes and stories are a form of verbal doctoring, a constructive and creative response to people's complaints, pain, and worries.

I have seen Dad take the tonic himself. Once about fifteen years ago when he was quite concerned about some serious business matters, we were talking in the living room, and he described grimly the impasse he seemed to be facing. Some minutes of pained silence went by. Dad slowly rose from his reading chair without a word, went upstairs and brought down a book of stories by a favorite humorist. Without any other comments, he began reading it aloud very expressively, and soon he was laughing and giving himself, and us, the mental space in which to regroup. It was a striking incident that I will never forget.

Come to think of it, there was actually one medical use for Dad's jokes that is very memorable, and that was for keeping you calm when he gave you a shot. Dad's nurse, Alene, was wonderful at administering nearly painless injections through speed and accuracy. But Dad had his own novel way, which was a clever kind of distraction technique.

He would first swab with alcohol the area to be injected while talking with you about some interesting matter. You might start to get tense and say something like, "I hope this isn't going to hurt . . ." and at that point Dad would quickly interrupt you with the start of a joke, using a forceful and comical voice:

"Say: how many letters do you pronounce in the word 'lamb'?" As soon as you started to think about the question, Dad would pinch and hold the

214

injection area very firmly, almost scaring you a little. Feeling that pinch, you would fear that even worse was coming. If you looked away and seemed alarmed, Dad would say, "Now don't you worry. Tell me about those letters!" and he would wait for your answer as though it had some importance to him.

After a second you would say, "Well, I think you pronounce only the first three letters, although this is probably some type of trick question." Dad would then look at you with approval and say, "Ah, very good! As you correctly stated, you only pronounce the L, A and M . . . the 'B' is silent, like the 'P' in swimming!" You would think half a second then start laughing – or groaning, depending on your opinion of the joke (he'd have another if you didn't like that one). About that time, you would feel Dad wiping the injection site again with a cotton swab and you would say, "Hey, did you give me the shot yet?" and he would say "You bet your life!" with a big smile, and in that second the both of you were as happy as could be.

Because of the pinch hold, you didn't notice the pain of the needle, which was small by comparison. And while you were distracted by the joke, Dad injected very fast and nonchalantly. So if you were looking away, you really had the illusion that the shot had never even happened!

I don't think I ever saw anyone else use this technique except Dad, and I can only say that this is a topic about which he should have spoken at medical meetings. He really should have gotten a patent on it (impossible of course), or at least coined the term, "The Dr. Murray Method" to designate the procedure.

We have never heard from Dad how he got in the habit of paying such close attention to humorous stories, but he has told us in this book about Aunt Lydia and her little black book of punch lines and memory prompts (Chapter 23) and how she would ask for jokes from him. Perhaps this was his start.

Dad has a special place in his humorous heart for farming folk and their outlook on life. When he, early-on, moved his practice out from downtown to what was then the edge of Lima, he began to take in a large percentage of patients from the country. He has expressed often his admiration for not only the wit of many farmers but also their skepticism, their frugality, and their bottom-line practical focus. He acquired a starter vocabulary of old-timer country expressions from his dad, who was a carpenter and raised on a farm on North Cole Street, and from his mom, who was also farm-reared. He has actively added to it throughout his career. Dad is one of the few people I know who could get an equal amount of joy from a virtuoso symphonic performance and from a really good rendition of "Here, Rattler, Here!"

Akin to his attachment to family farming, which seems to be vanishing rapidly from the American scene, is his nostalgia for the old times in general. He has, for many of us, a way of keeping those old days very interesting. Once as a kid, I got the whole seven-volume *McGuffey Readers* set, along with the *Webster's Blue-Backed Speller* from "Santa Claus." Was there any mystery in the fact that I later found myself doing college research papers on such topics as William Holmes McGuffey and Horace Mann?

Dad has been asked to be an after-dinner raconteur many times over the years, and he took his early material from the likes of then-young standup comic Andy Griffith and spoofer Stan Freeberg, not to mention Old Time Radio. He would often write out and memorize his remarks, and would deliver them with a characteristic cadence that would let you know at many points that you were being set up for the punch line.

Where does Dad get his humor refuelings? Well, he's an inveterate reader, as is Mom. But he has always also been an equally diligent radio listener, and always made good use of a lot of the drive time his work required of him.

He would start his day very early, and the radio helped him to rev up from the get-go. Dad's bathroom was the audio arena for many of his radio favorites, such as Don McNeil, The Grand Ole Opry, Karl Haas, Renfro Valley Gathering, J. P. McCarthy, and Bud Guest. Dad enjoyed the toned-down humor (usually "groaner" jokes) of the Don McNeil show, and it probably gave him material suitable for entertaining his older patients, of whom he was very fond and, to whom he usually gave a lot of extra time and attention. He was always a loyal listener of WJR, Detroit, and greatly enjoyed interview programs, such as the daily "Focus" program with J. P. McCarthy.

Beyond humor and events, Dad also had a liking for story features on the radio that created a mood, such as Mike Whorf's "Kaleidoscope" program on WJR and Karl Haas's "Adventures in Good Music." Dad liked to catch Golden Age Radio when he could, too. He bought LPs for us to hear at home of

217

Edward R. Morrow ("I Can Hear it Now"), of stories by Sam Levinson, and of Charles Laughton narrating dramatic readings of *Treasure Island* and *Moby Dick*. And he himself used to nudge us to laughter by his fractured, melodramatic recitations before a blazing winter fire of "The Raven," "The Rime of the Ancient Mariner," "Who Has Seen the Wind?", "The Song of Hiawatha," "The Village Blacksmith" and "The Midnight Ride of Paul Revere."

Television had its role to play, too, and Dad would descend in the morning to take in for later repeating the witticisms of Willard Scott. One example that I always remember caught Dad's fancy was when Willard paid birthday tribute to a potato farmer who was 100 years old and, holding out a big potato, said, "Sir, this spud's for you!"

At night, Dad liked watching the antics of Chuck Osborn on WIMA (later, WLIO) TV when he would do the local ads. Chuck would start talking about lawn furniture, standing alone on a blank set, and all of a sudden a beach chair would come lobbing in at him and he would have to leap aside because the studio guys would darned near hit him with it. He'd catch the chair, nonchalantly hold it up, talk about this fine quality chair from Rink's Bargain City and then throw it back, as though this was the way people always behaved on TV. He'd resume talking and pretty soon two loaves of Holsum Soft Twist Bread would fly at him. He'd grab them and start talking about Pangle's Master Markets or Clyde Evans Stores and then a big 16-oz Coke would barrel in. He would betray the minimum of nervousness but the station guys were obviously playing some kind of game of chicken and the viewers got to be in on it. You felt like you knew them all and they were your buddies. Dad got quite a kick out of Chuck, as did all the family, and for awhile, Chuck was even Dad's patient.

But let us return to the main subject under examination.

Whether stories are involved or not, it would be difficult not to notice that, even as a speaker in common situations, Dad is a rare individual in his gift for oral composition. He has a redoubtable command of English vocabulary and a talent for using it with stylistic flair. I honestly don't know anyone who regularly uses English in such a discriminating, apt and *poetic* way as does Dad. Perhaps this explains his huge enjoyment of Rex Harrison playing Professor Henry Higgins in the musical, *My Fair Lady*. Dad was a clever and quick composer of many humorous poems that he would insert into birthday cards or use as treasure hunt clues. Mom (who is half-Irish) would read these and absolutely *roar* with laughter and the kids would stand around semi-comprehending and smile and giggle.

I feel sorry that, in these written stories, those who don't know Dad personally may miss ever hearing the colorful extemporaneous wit that makes so many of his spoken comments so ingenious and fun. He is a very witty man. It would be a long book indeed that would chronicle the small episodes in which an unexpected side comment, barb, impersonation, characterization or dramatization by Dad has transformed a gloomy or dull atmosphere into complete hilarity, as if by magic. I feel that Dad gets bored with the dullness of a lot of common talk and he uses language in such a way as to keep himself and

219

others in an interesting game. Dad is a good writer, but he is an even better speaker.

Akin to the fact that Dad actually *uses* a high percentage of the words he knows is that he is very given to *details*. This can be a little vexing to some at times (not that I would mean *Mom* here) because he often exhibits a precision or density of technical fill-in that is not called for or demanded in a situation. However, I feel that Dad is very sensitive to atmosphere and that the right details and terms of art in their totality create a vivid backdrop for him as he narrates. He likes to set his stage. Details of brand names, plant species, part sizes and the names of miscellaneous people met along the way are all important in his universe.

Moreover, I am sure he has found over time that various listeners may get unexpected flashes from some of these details and that they express appreciation for them. I think it is similar to what I run into in teaching computer software classes, which is what I do professionally. Every program offers many more features than can be covered effectively in a beginner's class. But every time I have played down some "minor" feature, such as how to make your text font a different color or how to get the program to print off onto a non-standard size of paper, somebody at the back of class yells, "Hey, what do you mean, that feature isn't important? I use it every day! It's great! It saves me so much time!"

(Dear me! – did I go into too much detail about *that*?)

Besides these explanations for Dad's occasional nerdiness, there is another: Dad worked all the time. And in his diagnosis and care of patients, it was always important to notice the most minute facts. All the relevant findings from an exam or during treatment were not going to be pointed out to you by outsiders and if you missed anything important, it was your fault. Dad often seemed like Watson of the Sherlock Holmes stories, who was in constant peril of having Sherlock point out to him some small but critical fact of a situation that could have botched the case if not caught. So it was probably hard at times for Dad to turn off the habit of clinically-precise reporting, especially working the long hours he did.

Within his field of work, if I may say so, I can wear witness that Dad has always been perceived by his friends, patients, colleagues and drug reps to be a supreme medical generalist. This is a high distinction indeed that I use advisedly. And if I may divulge something that you'd never hear from Dad: in his recertifications for Family Medicine, Dad always tested in the top third of the qualifying physicians.

He is, in fact, interested in all facets of life, and curious about nearly everything. But one subject was always supreme: Dad *loved* medicine! His patients always held no end of fascination for him and were, as he labored in his orderly, rectangular office building at 2875 West Elm Street, a window to the world like no other. When he first began his years in private practice, a surgeon friend helped Dad and his partner, Dr. Grannis, get the loan to build their office. This gentleman, Dr. Charles H. Leach, was kind enough to advance them the $10,000 they needed for their down payment. In a kind of jovial send-off, he said to them

221

of general practice, "You are going to be on a front row seat in the Greatest Show on Earth." Dad never forgot, nor doubted, this assessment his whole career.

Dad liked to refer to drug reps as "detail men" (their own professional term), and I'm sure that the real fun for Dad was always in discussing the details. No doubt very much was always learned there, at that level.

Nonetheless, Dad has also had, by contrast, a definite habit of brushing aside excessive details that could amount to so much mental debris when it got down to the actual welfare of his patients, for whom he felt a pointed responsibility, a fierce loyalty and genuine affection. At medical conventions he might excuse one of his "What's the bottom line for our practice?" questions asked of an academic medical researcher by saying "If you will please excuse an ignorant question on behalf of us butter-and-egg men out in the hinterlands, what do we actually DO with this information?"

When it comes to a story, Dad has always taken the logic and build of a narration seriously. When we, his kids, were very small, we would ask Dad to make up stories, and he would tell imaginary tales that often involved some kid or other (like us) getting scared of something and running away. After suitable suspense and buildup, Dad would make the sound of the kid screaming as the story would have the kid bolting away from the scene in fright, and we would all just laugh fit to bust. But I would notice that Dad would always take a moment to think about the story before he would tell us, as though he wanted to deliver quality. He wouldn't just barrel in, assuming his chosen punch line was enough. There was planning involved, and I remember thinking that if you needed to stop and think before you even just told a funny story, then thinking something through beforehand might be good in a lot of other things, too.

One Sunday about thirty-five years ago, after dinner in the dining room, Dad sat down at the typewriter in a creative mood and began composing. We were surprised at what a good typist he was (as, you may remember, he *most enthusiastically* was for the Graves Registration Department in the Army!). He quickly wrote a funny impromptu story about a little frog. He joked that he would later write his memoirs someday. I had a funny feeling that he really would, though at the time I'm sure he was only kidding.

Dad asked me to help him organize and copy-edit some of his material for this book, and it has indeed been a high pleasure for me to become so well-acquainted with aspects of his life story that I hitherto did not know well. Mom, my brother, Scott, and sisters, Cindy and Betsy, have heard perhaps half of these stories before (actually, *many* times before) but, unfortunately, usually in snatches and overheard remarks made to other relatives. Now and then Dad would try to brief us on his past, too, in the midst of his hectic schedule, but so often a quiet moment for a story would be cut short by a telephone call summoning him away abruptly to deliver a baby or make a house call.

Now at last, we have the Main Stories, settled and done, in a form that won't run away, no matter how urgent the ephemera of our daily preoccupations may seem, and no matter how far we may roam in space and time from the Good Old Days in Lima. Dad has passed on a wonderful legacy of his most cherished stories to us.

With this book goes the hope that the slumbering coals of nostalgia in the hearts of many folks -- far beyond just our particular family or old local neighborhood -- may recognize their call to awaken. May Dad's readers relive the old days again, and feel the love for those they hold dear more fully and strongly than ever!

38.   More to Come!

It is my hope to gradually bring out new stories over time. Some of the topics I am mulling over as possi-bilities are:

--High School During WW II
--College and Medical School Adventures
--The Ups and Downs of Medical Internship
--Changes in Medicine Through the Years

Please check now and then to see future material at:
www.explain.com/newstories

I always enjoy hearing from friends and readers and I like to hear your memories and stories, too. I hope that this book will be a stimulus for other members of our Shell Point Memoirs class to pursue printing up their stories for their families.

Please contact me at:
11310 Oakmont Court
Ft. Myers, FL 33908
(239) 466-5895
e-mail: dukepollyfm@webtv.net

Thank you for reminiscing with me.

--Duke Murray

Biographical Sketch
(or, *Just the Facts, Please!*)

Dr. Emmett Murray, known as Duke to friends and family, practiced family medicine in Lima, Ohio from 1953 till 1995, when he retired. He and his wife, Polly, then moved to Ft. Myers, Florida to the Woodlands, a residential area in the Shell Point Village retirement community.

He was born at home on Hazel Avenue in Lima in 1925 to Faye and Emmett Murray, the youngest of four children. His father was a construction foreman and carpenter and his mother, a former candy-maker and an excellent cook, was at home full-time. Both had been raised on farms and enjoyed Duke's pursuit of adventure as he helped with chores on his aunt and uncle's farm.

Duke Murray developed an interest in hunting and sporting dogs and found success in dog shows with his prize beagle, Ace. He worked at many jobs while growing up and thought he would continue working after high school rather than go on to college. However his brother, Marvin, and his neighbor, Ruth Creviston, insisted that he attend college. Because of his experiences on the farm and with his dogs, he decided to become a veterinarian.

This plan was disrupted when, after less than a year in college as an ROTC freshman, he was called into active military duty in 1944. He was trained by the Army as an X-ray technician, and then sent to France where he worked in several Army hospitals during his two-and-a-half-year tour of duty. During this time, a chance remark by an Army doctor changed his destiny. The doctor, hearing about Duke's plans for vet school, said, "Why don't you try medicine?" and told him he thought he'd be good at it. After the war, Duke Murray changed his Ohio State major to pre-med, and the die was cast.

During medical school he continued to employ his X-ray skills as a part-time technician, and he met someone else on the job who had been taught to take X-rays, a medical secretary from Columbus named Pauline List. They shared a sense of humor, among many other things, and in 1949 were married in a double-ceremony with Pauline's twin sister, Kathleen, who married Daniel Susil. Duke and Polly had their first son, Scott, in 1952, who later completed pre-med at Ohio State like his dad and then went on not only to become a physician but also to marry one (Dr. Nancy Winters) as well.

After Duke's graduation in Columbus, he and Polly moved to his home town of Lima and he completed his internship at St. Rita's hospital. The couple had three more children, Robin (Robb), Cynthia Ann (Cindy) and Betsy. Dr. Murray opened his office practice in 1953 on the day his second son, Robb, was born. He began in practice with Drs. Bill Grannis and Bill Foxx, then added Ken Burns, and later practiced in sole partnership with Dr. Gene Wright. From day one, he highly esteemed the sterling services of nurse, Alene Grothouse, from Delphos, who provided very intelligent, capable, knowledgeable, effective and dedicated assistance for the entire duration of his practice.

To supplement his office practice, Dr. Murray worked part time at BLH (formerly the Lima Locomotive Works) as the plant doctor for 25 years, from 1954 to 1979, and later continued his involvement with occupational medicine in helping Dr. A. C. Reed to set up a plant clinic at Crown Control in New Bremen, Ohio in the early 1990s.

Dr. and Mrs. Murray were supporters of many Lima cultural and professional organizations such as the Cotillion Club, the Lima Symphony, Encore Theater, the Lima Elks Lodge, and the Lima Medical Auxiliary. Pauline (Polly) was active in the Lotus Club, the League of Women Voters, and the Red Cross. Dr. Murray served for a time on the Consistory of Calvary UCC, and he was elected to the Lima City Board of Education in 1962 and served as President from 1965-1970. He was Chief of Staff at Lima Memorial Hospital for a two-year term during the 1980s.

Dr. Murray's boyhood hobbies of hunting and dog shows were gradually replaced by fishing, handball, tennis and, much later, gardening. He has remained an inveterate storyteller, humorist, and something of a mimic as well. Both Dr. and Mrs. Murray are devoted readers, and each reads aloud to the other quite often. In Ft. Myers, they enjoy attending the Southwest Florida Symphony programs and numerous other plays and shows. They are quite active in the Current Affairs discussion group at Shell Point, and both attend meetings of the Tamiami Tale Tellers (TTT) Club, the weekly coffee hour at the Woodlands, services at the Village Church and, of course, their Memoirs class.

Duke and Polly love to talk and reminisce with patients and friends from over the years and may be reached at (239) 466-5895 or at dukepollyfm@webtv.net or at 11310 Oakmont Court, Ft. Myers, FL 33908.

--Robb Murray

Neat Things
a Kid Could Learn
in the 1930s

(Guess the answer, then look it up!)

- How do you crack 500 walnuts at once? (page 75)
- How can a burglar alarm backfire? (page 144)
- What does the circus offer besides the show? (page 59)
- Is cigarette smoking really so hazardous? (pages 106-107)
- How do you sell a boring newspaper on the street? (page 80)
- What *won't* catch night crawlers? (pages 75-76)
- How can a present be more fun that comes broken?
     (pages 157-158)
- Do you really need a stove to cook eggs? (pages 10-11)
- How do you keep ice cream from spoiling? (page 86)
- What can you listen to if your radio isn't working? (page 27)
- Can just anyone succeed in small business? (page 41)
- Are typing lessons really worth the time? (page 177)
- What do you pack when you report to the Army? (page 168)
- Where is a hunting dog's "flag" kept? (page 92)
- What is the danger in listening to spooky radio shows? (page 130)
- How do you know when it's time to go in for supper? (page 16)
- What makes a chunk of ice dangerous? (page 101)
- How can a screen door be a double-weapon? (page 17)
- What's the best way to remember jokes? (page 132)
- What game starts on the ground but ends in the air? (page 67)
- What is "Decoration Day"? (page 154)
- How do you know if your valentine has a crush on you?
     (pages 55-56)

ISBN 141200981-2

9 781412 009812